UPCYCLE

LAURENCE KING

Published in 2015 by Laurence King Publishing Ltd
361–373 City Road
London EC1V 1LR
United Kingdom
Tel: +44 20 7841 6900
Fax: +44 20 7841 6910
e-mail: enquiries@laurenceking.com
www.laurenceking.com

A catalogue record for this book is available from the British Library.

ISBN: 978-1-78067-600-5

Design by Eleanor Ridsdale
Line drawings by Lily Tennant

Printed in China

FSC
www.fsc.org

MIX
Paper from
responsible sources
FSC® C008047

Rebecca Proctor

UPCYCLE

24 Sustainable DIY Projects

Laurence King Publishing

CONTENTS

06
Introduction

10
Reading Lamp by HILLSIDEOUT

16
**Morgan Rope Mat
by Sophie Aschauer**

20
**Strawberry-Box Bench
by Henry Baumann**

24
Marine Light by Nir Meiri

28
TetraBox Lamp by Ed Chew

38
**Strand-Board Table
by Ryan Frank**

44
Unplugged by Asia Piaścik

52
**Copper-Pipe Clothing Rail
by Madelynn Furlong**

58
Plastic Blooms by Sarah Turner

64
**Cross-Stitch Chair
by Cintia Gonzalez**

68
F.aid by Mischer'Traxler Studio

72
**Wooden Wall Sculpture
by Martin Gerstenberger**

76
Pixelate by Rachel Parker

82
**Pallet Window Shelf
by Christopher Berry**

88
**Wine-Box Ottoman
by Chloe Edwards**

96
Rag Rug by Angela Weissenfels

100
**Star Cushion
by Place de Bleu**

108
**Bottle Vase
by Stella Melgrati**

114
**Carpenter-Square Shelf
by Fabien Cappello**

120
Crate Stool by Segev Moisa

126
**Hunter Leather-Label Rug
by Joanne Crocker**

130
**Loofah Screen
by Fernando Laposse**

136
**Palitos Lamp
by Sergio Mendoza**

140
**DIY Panton Chair
by Peter Jakubik**

INTRODUCTION
DISCARDED TO DESIRABLE

Upcycling is a great way to create desirable and unique designs from discarded items and basic materials, changing their purpose and giving them a new life. While recycling merely allows objects to be used again in some way, upcycling aims to increase their original value, resulting in products that are innovative and stylish, yet often make no secret of their humble origins.

Designers may have different reasons for working in this way, but perhaps the primary motivation of the upcycling movement is the challenge of pitting innovation and creativity against the excesses of disposable culture. By exploring imaginative ways of using existing objects, instead of continually buying new ones, we can make a stand, however small, against wasteful consumerism and mass production, while, hopefully, having some fun in the process.

There are environmental benefits too. Finding new uses for discarded objects not only cuts down on landfill, but reduces demand on virgin resources and the energy used to extract them. Many designers feel it is no longer desirable — or justifiable — to create products without eco credentials in a world already filled with decades' worth of countless consumer goods; upcycling offers the perfect solution.

In fact, the instant sense of history and life which pre-used materials bring to new products is frequently preferable to the soulless nature of pristine materials. Taking this a step further, designers are often drawn to the notion of contributing to the 'story' of an object by opening a fresh chapter in its life, rather than throwing it away.

While upcycling with new materials may seem less appealing, and lacks the associated eco benefits, it has the great attraction of being cheap, as it usually focuses on humble components such as household objects and industrial supplies. This results in a unique kind of magic, where simple materials transcend their intended uses to take on a loftier purpose.

One such project is Madelynn Furlong's Copper-Pipe Clothing Rail (page 52), which uses ordinary plumbing components to create a desirable piece of furniture. Copper pipe is usually hidden away in walls and floors, but it is a versatile material with an attractive appearance that develops a nice patina with age. Not only does her design encourage us to reconsider the intended role of materials, it might also make us rethink the way we store clothes, showing off our favourite pieces, rather than hiding them in a dark cupboard.

Sophie Aschauer's Morgan Rope Mat (page 16) takes a different approach, creating something useful from rope that was once very expensive but has become almost worthless. Although old sailing rope loses the vital element of strength, it is still hardwearing, weatherproof and aesthetically appealing, and hints at unknown travels and adventure — qualities that are all neatly exploited in this new incarnation.

Taking on the challenge of upcycling materials with no value at all, Henry Baumann's Strawberry-Box Bench (page 20) finds a use for the thousands of wooden crates discarded or burnt at markets every day. By breaking them down into their basic components, Henry has discovered a set of useful geometric building blocks with the potential to create substantial products at virtually no expense.

Like many projects in this book, the design of the Strawberry-Box Bench need not be followed to the letter, but can simply be taken as inspiration or a starting-point for your own unique project. What these examples all aspire to do, however, is to encourage seeing potential in unlikely places and to demonstrate that a bit of creativity and a few simple tools are really all you need to begin upcycling.

I hope you enjoy the projects featured and feel inspired to try to recreate them yourself. The instructions are intended to be as foolproof as possible, although some basic experience in making will certainly be useful. As ever, practice makes perfect, so if your first attempt at upcycling turns out differently than expected, keep practising! And remember that all the designers featured in this book have been experimenting and honing their craft for years.

READING LAMP
BY HILLSIDEOUT

HILLSIDEOUT is a joint project between Andrea Zambelli and Nat Wilms, based in Bologna, Italy. The duo aim to create furnishings that embrace art, design and the antique, characterized by their melding of vintage and modern materials using contemporary techniques.

Andrea is a furniture restorer with a passion for the unique properties of high-quality, recycled Italian wood, while Nat is an artist with a background in sculpture and multimedia. Their joint designs often contain historical 'layers' in conjunction with modern transparent materials, such as resin or Perspex, exemplifying their desire to combine 'the poetic with the innovative'.

Many of their designs start from a found object with a previous life, such as a wheel, a drawer or a lock. HILLSIDEOUT believe this attention to history and 'personality' gives an upcycled product a depth that is absent in new products.

The Reading Lamp is a perfect example of their aesthetic, combining a modern lamp fitting and plastic with recycled wood. It would be a good way to recycle small scraps of different types of timber, or an unwanted piece of furniture made of quality materials.

HILLSIDEOUT rate the degree of difficulty of this project as about five on a scale of one to ten and recommend an unhurried, precise approach. It is also important to allow the glue to cure fully, so it may be best to attempt the lamp over a few days, rather than in a single session.

www.hillsideout.com

READING LAMP

MATERIALS
↑ Sheet of graph paper
↑ Scrap wood
↑ Wood glue
↑ Lamp holder with screws
↑ 2 Perspex (Plexiglas) rods
↑ Bolts and wing nuts, or screws
↑ Natural wax
↑ Electrical cable, switch (optional) and socket
↑ LED bulb of max 7W (equivalent to 50W) with GU10 connection

TOOLS
↑ Handsaw
↑ Drill
↑ Large vice or clamp
↑ Small screwdriver
↑ File
↑ Sandpaper

HILLSIDEOUT's example is made of handcrafted alder and nut wood, Perspex, brass screws and an electrical light system with an LED lamp of 7W. Dimensions of the final lamp are approximately L25 x D20 x H60cm (L10 x D8 x H23½in).

1

Sketch a design for your Reading Lamp on graph paper, then cut the slices of wood using the handsaw in the dimensions you need. Alternatively, you could cut a selection of pieces and assemble them spontaneously.

2

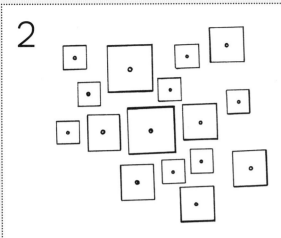

A hole wide enough to run electrical cable through the stack can be drilled after assembly. However, if you don't have a long enough drill bit, drill through each wood slice individually now.

3

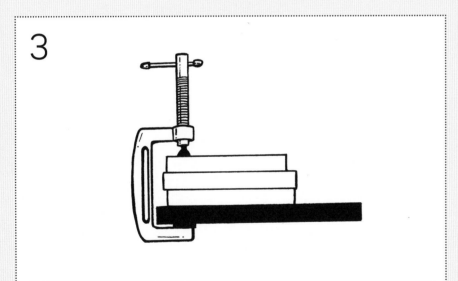

To make the candlestick-shaped column, start from the bottom, gluing the pieces together one by one. Wipe off any excess glue immediately with a damp cloth. Press them together firmly using a large clamp or vice, or stand the stack upright and balance a weight on top of it.

4

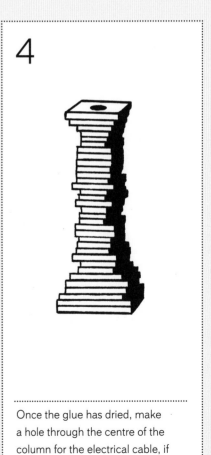

Once the glue has dried, make a hole through the centre of the column for the electrical cable, if you haven't done so already.

5

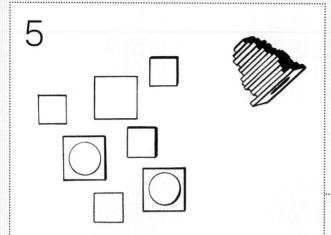

Make the bell-shaped second piece, using the same construction technique as before. However, you will need to make a bigger hole this time to accommodate the lamp holder and bulb. If you cannot make a large enough hole, you can use thinner pieces to make four-sided frames for each slice. Check the size of these parts against the lamp you want to use before assembly.

6

Put the lamp holder inside and fix it with 2 screws.

7

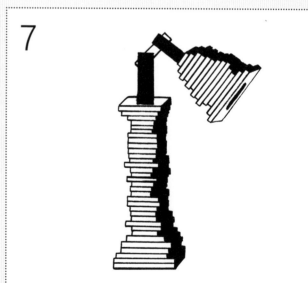

Connect the candlestick base and bell-shaped lamp using 2 Perspex rods, or wooden ones if you prefer. If you want a range of movement, you will need to make holes at the end of the rods and pin them with bolts and wing nuts. If not, you can fix them in place with glue and/or screws.

8

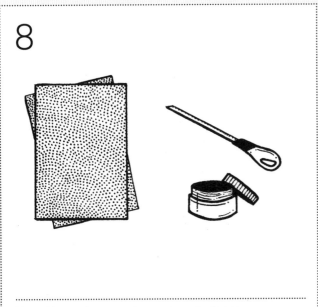

Use a file, sandpaper and natural wax for finishing.

9

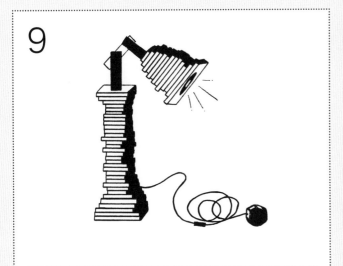

Fit the electrical cable with a socket and add a switch if you like. Put the bulb into the lamp, choosing white or yellow light as you prefer, and enjoy your self-made Reading Lamp.

MORGAN ROPE MAT
BY SOPHIE ASCHAUER

The inspiration behind New York-based company SerpentSea came from a book of sailor's knots, picked up on a sailing trip to Nantucket Island. Austrian designer Sophie Aschauer was struck by the beauty and complexity of these traditional patterns and felt compelled to incorporate them into woven mats.

On sailing boats, reliable rope is essential. Anything less than perfect must be replaced, leaving an abundance of discarded rope in a vast range of colours. This surplus provides Sophie with the perfect source material for upcycling into her intricate handwoven creations. She has never had to buy any new material and works exclusively with rope that would otherwise be thrown away. Since the rope is designed for use in harsh ocean environments, the mats are ideal for use both indoors and out. According to the designer, they also work well as bathmats as they feel very nice under bare feet.

This project follows Sophie's Morgan design, named after the notorious pirate Henry Morgan who terrorized the Spanish Main in the seventeenth century. The pattern uses what is traditionally known as a prolong knot — so named because the design can be prolonged by adding more and more rope until the desired result is achieved. Ideally, it should be made from about 50 metres (165 feet) of 9–10mm (⅜in) nylon marine or mountaineering rope. It is possible to use thicker material, but anything thinner is not recommended. The process takes Sophie about four hours per rug, so allow at least this to complete the project.

www.serpentsea.com

MORGAN ROPE MAT

MATERIALS
↑ 50m (165ft) nylon marine or
  mountaineering rope, at least
  9–10mm (⅜in) in diameter

TOOLS
↑ Hot knife or strong needle

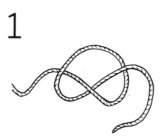

Form a loose knot at one end of the
rope. Leave a tail about 1m (3ft)
long on the right-hand side, and the
remaining slack rope to the left.

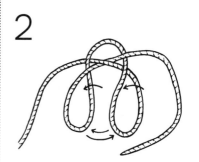

Gently pull down on the loops at the
bottom, flipping them to the left,
as shown.

Now cross the loops, laying the left
one on top of the right. Take the tail
end and weave it through the knot
as shown.

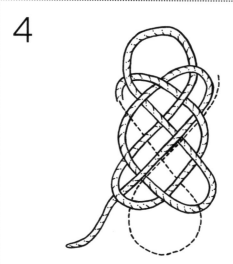

Now take the slack end and weave it diagonally from the
upper left towards the lower right. Pull the rope all the way
through and continue weaving back to the top as shown,
adjusting the rope to resemble the diagram. The first round
is now complete.

5

Take the remaining slack and follow the path of the first round, staying parallel to the woven rope and pulling the rope through after each pass. Different shades of rope can be used at the end of each round to create a more colourful mat, as long as the ends are all sealed together (see Step 7). Continue doubling and tripling up until the desired width is reached. Six rounds makes a well-proportioned mat.

6

Once the weaving is complete, the mat will probably look a bit irregular. Start at the beginning of the rope and work along the entire length, making it tighter and tighter until the desired form has been reached.

7

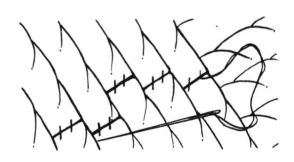

To close the ends, cut off the excess rope and, ideally, melt them together with a hot knife. If this isn't possible, they can also be sewn together and the frayed edges tidied up with a lighter.

STRAWBERRY-BOX BENCH
BY HENRY BAUMANN

Henry Baumann's Netherlands-based design studio focuses on giving new life to unwanted materials. This allows the German designer to save objects that would otherwise end up as waste and to take advantage of materials that are available for free.

However, Henry's main incentive is not to reduce waste, but to accept the challenge of unlocking the hidden potential in these materials. He tasks himself with reinstating meaning to objects that have lost their original purpose, not by substantially changing the material itself, but merely by highlighting its positive qualities.

He is particularly fascinated by items that are available in large quantities yet receive little attention, such as cable drums, or the strawberry boxes used in this design. The concept is based on a project called 130, which was constructed from 130 strawberry crates collected from Maastricht's fruit market. These are usually thrown away, but Henry found they could be dismantled to yield a selection of versatile building blocks.

This project uses just eight crates as a starting-point, although it can be expanded without limit. The individual steps of the project are relatively simple; according to Henry, the main thing — as with all artisanal labour — is to enjoy the process.

www.henrybaumann.de

STRAWBERRY-BOX BENCH

MATERIALS
↑ 8 wooden strawberry boxes
↑ Wood glue

TOOLS
↑ Pliers
↑ Clamps

1

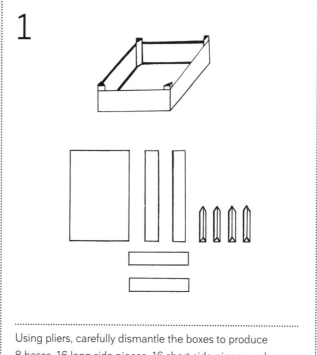

Using pliers, carefully dismantle the boxes to produce 8 bases, 16 long side pieces, 16 short side pieces and 32 elbows (the corner joints).

2

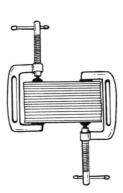 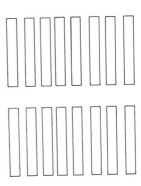

Assemble the 16 long side pieces into a continuous zigzag or concertina form by applying glue to opposite sides of the ends of each piece. Clamp the pieces together neatly, wiping any excess glue with a damp cloth, and let dry.

3

Pull the concertina form into a circular shape, glue the beginning and end and clamp them together. The result is a sturdy cylinder.

4

Glue an elbow between each of the 8 spaces at the ends for reinforcement. Further elbows can be added to create a variety of geometric patterns.

5

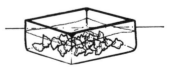

Tear the bases of the boxes into little pieces and soak them in water for about two weeks. The material produced can then be mixed with glue and used to fill any spaces in the pattern.

MARINE LIGHT
BY NIR MEIRI

Nir Meiri's Tel Aviv studio takes a highly individual approach to the design of everyday objects. Nir particularly enjoys employing unusual natural materials, such as desert sand, plant pots and seaweed, in new and innovative ways. Shaping them into clean-cut forms, his products aim to explore the relationship between the domesticated and the untamed. His reason for recycling and using natural materials is simple: he believes this to be the best way to avoid contributing to today's abundance of waste.

Ancient cultures are known to have appreciated and utilized the diverse properties of seaweed for millennia, and today it is cultivated and harvested on a commercial scale. Ingredients for toothpaste, ice-cream and fertilizers are extracted from this versatile material and, as a result of a growing interest driven by environmental concerns, seaweed has found its way into a growing number of applications, such as bio-fuels.

Nir offers a striking alternative by using it as the primary component in a piece of contemporary domestic furniture. The Marine Light uses raw seaweed to create a design that is reminiscent of the sea itself. When the lamp is lit, the shiny film created from the seaweed forms an algae-like underwater projection. The skill level required for this project is very low, but it does require a lot of patience.

www.nirmeiri.com

MARINE LIGHT

MATERIALS
↑ **Metal lampshade frame**
↑ **Fresh seaweed**
↑ **Bio-resin**

TOOLS
↑ **Brush**

1

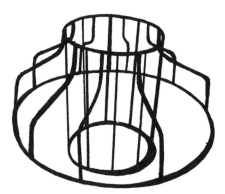

Source a metal frame from an unwanted lampshade in the shape you want, or create your own frame from wire or coat-hangers.

2

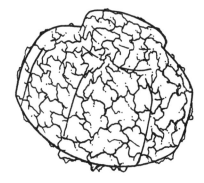

Drape the shade all over with strips of fresh seaweed until it is completely covered.

3

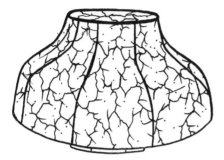

Allow the seaweed to dry for a few hours in the sun, where it will shrink and harden over the form of the frame.

4

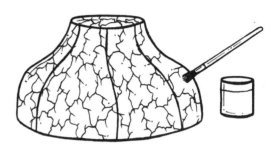

When the seaweed is completely dry, brush bio-resin gently over the lampshade and let it dry. For best results, repeat Steps 2–4 once or twice, using more seaweed and bio-resin.

5

Once the shade is dry, hang it on your chosen light and enjoy the natural, aquatic glow!

TETRABOX LAMP
BY ED CHEW

Ed Chew is the founder of an architectural firm based in Malaysia. Although most of his time is spent on his professional career, he indulges himself in DIY projects whenever possible. Ed likes to think of his designs as artworks created to raise public awareness of the possibilities of upcycling discarded items into useful everyday products. His projects are particularly accessible as he prefers easily sourced materials, which can be worked without the use of heavy tools or machinery.

Ed's interest in upcycling began when he was a student in Australia, in response to the high cost of living for an international student with limited funds. His first project was a desk made from a discarded solid-wood door and the satisfying result inspired him to fill his room with handmade shelves, a bed frame and a sofa base, all made from milk crates.

The TetraBox Lamp, which won first prize in Inhabit's Bright Ideas lighting design competition, is an intricate, futuristic design made from little more than empty juice cartons cut into strips. The strips are folded into simple triangles, which are then assembled without using any adhesive to create a geodesic sphere.

Despite its complex appearance, Ed insists that the construction process is as simple as making (a large number of!) paper planes. Once you have learned the basic principles, it is possible to manipulate the design to create a variety of sizes and forms.

www.edchew.my

TETRABOX LAMP

MATERIALS
- ↑ Approximately 450 x 250ml (8oz) Tetra Pak cartons
- ↑ Wire pot-stand (the type used to support a cooking pot on a gas burner), or fitting adapted from a lampshade
- ↑ Polypropylene sheet (e.g. from a plastic milk container)
- ↑ Light fitting with bulb holder

TOOLS
- ↑ Ruler
- ↑ Paper-clips

1

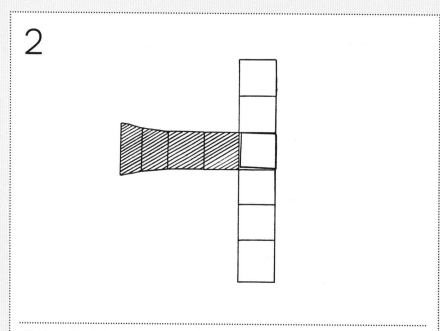

Cut open and flatten the cartons, wiping off any liquid or stickiness. Mark the cartons as shown and cut the strips to the required sizes. A strips are 2.1cm (⅘in) wide and B strips are 1.8cm (⁷⁄₁₀in) wide.

2

Divide an A strip into squares, using the width of another A strip as a guide for the first square. Repeat the folding process until there are 6 squares. Don't worry that the last square will often be slightly small.

3

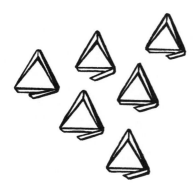

Now fold the strip into a double-layered triangle. Repeat this process until you have 6 triangles.

4

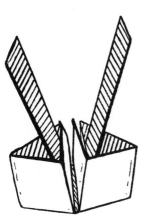

Join 2 triangles by placing the sides with the loose ends together and inserting the end of a folded tie strip (B) into each one.

5

Cut the ends of the tie strip so they are short enough to fold and tuck neatly against the loose ends of the triangles.

6

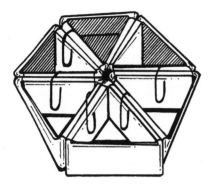

Repeat this process to join all 6 triangles. Using paper-clips to hold the triangles together, arrange them into a hexagon.

7

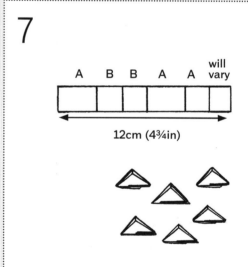

To make a pentagonal module, follow the same folding process but use slightly different measurements to make non-equilateral triangles. Place the longer edges outwards when two triangles are joined together. You need 6 of these.

8

Knot these edges
together

Pentagon in
centre

When you have 5 hexagonal modules, they can be joined
with tie strips to make a cluster module. Close the loop with
a knotted tie strip, as shown top, and secure a pentagon in
the centre of each cluster.

Equilateral triangles

Hexagonal modules

Cluster modules

Pentagons within cluster modules

Make 6 cluster modules and fill the gaps between clusters with 20 hexagonal modules (striped) and 30 equilateral triangles (dotted) as shown to form a half-sphere.

10

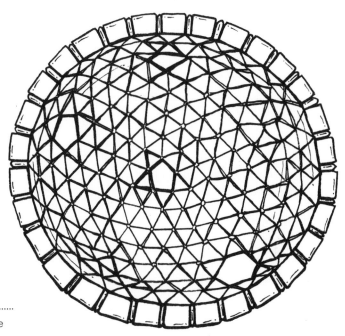

Repeat the previous steps to make the second half-sphere.

11

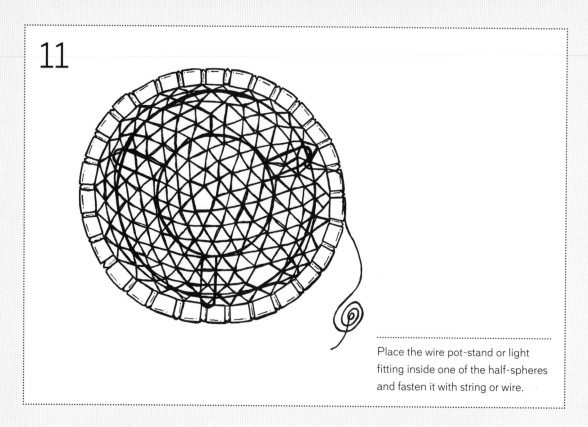

Place the wire pot-stand or light fitting inside one of the half-spheres and fasten it with string or wire.

12

Place the spheres together, removing a few triangles to allow a hand to fit through, and knot them together with tie strips.

13

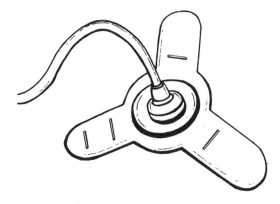

Cut a sheet of polypropylene into shape, ensuring it fits neatly onto the pot-stand. Now fix it to the light fitting.

14

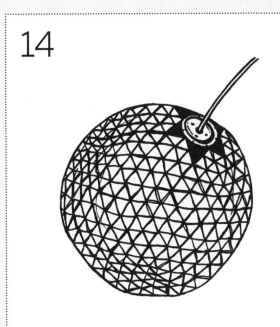

Fasten the completed light fitting into the pot-stand inside the shade to complete the TetraBox Lamp.

STRAND-BOARD TABLE
BY RYAN FRANK

Ryan Frank is a furniture designer based in London and Barcelona, who specializes in what he describes as 'edgy, free-range furniture, with sustainability built in as standard'.

When Ryan creates his designs he considers their capacity to use recycled materials or be recycled themselves, the social implications of extracting raw materials and the efficiency of the production process. He believes that including these ideals in a design philosophy from the start, rather than tacking them on at the end, constitutes a true step towards 'green' design. Ryan's extremely varied output of eccentric and experimental designs — from chairs upholstered in fabric scraps to corrugated iron room-dividing screens — is characterized by a diverse use of materials, many of which are associated with far humbler applications.

This project employs a single sheet of OSB (oriented strand board), a cheap material made from shredded wood compressed with adhesive. OSB is commonly used in the building industry, hidden away in floors, roofs and walls, but is also often seen covering up broken shop windows or creating walls around construction sites. As a result, it can frequently be found discarded in skips (dumpsters), or bought inexpensively from a hardware shop.

This design leaves very little waste from a sheet and is held together with the minimum of fixings. It could also be customized to work in different sizes, but make sure the tabletop is large enough to cover the legs before you start cutting!

www.ryanfrank.net

STRAND-BOARD TABLE

MATERIALS
↑ Sheet of 18mm (¾in) OSB
  (oriented strand board), L2440 x
  W1220mm (L88 x W48in)
↑ Screws

TOOLS
↑ Long ruler
↑ Saw
↑ Sandpaper
↑ Drill
↑ Screwdriver

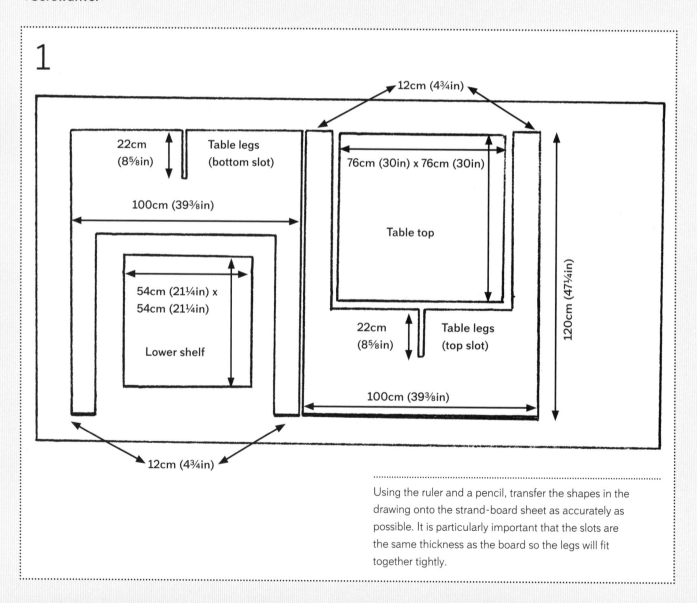

1

12cm (4¾in)

22cm (8⅝in) Table legs (bottom slot)

100cm (39⅜in)

76cm (30in) x 76cm (30in)

Table top

54cm (21¼in) x 54cm (21¼in)

Lower shelf

120cm (47¼in)

22cm (8⅝in) Table legs (top slot)

100cm (39⅜in)

12cm (4¾in)

Using the ruler and a pencil, transfer the shapes in the drawing onto the strand-board sheet as accurately as possible. It is particularly important that the slots are the same thickness as the board so the legs will fit together tightly.

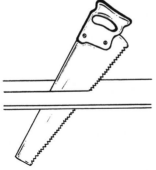

Using a saw, carefully cut the pieces out from the sheet. Smooth any rough edges with sandpaper.

3

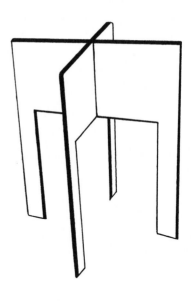

Slot the table legs together and stand them on the floor.

4

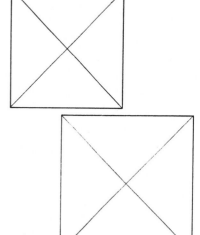

Draw a faint cross from corner to corner on the rougher side of the tabletop and shelf.

5

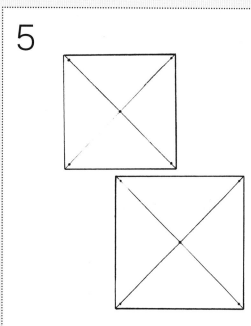

Drill screw holes 10cm (4in) in from each corner and a hole in the centre.

6

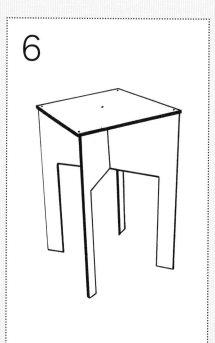

Place the tabletop board into position, cross side down, making sure it is central and the holes line up over the legs. Drill through the holes into the legs and insert the screws. Be sure to drill into the middle of the edge of the legs to reduce the risk of splitting the board.

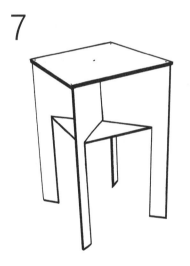

7

Repeat the previous step with the lower shelf, screwing it beneath the table legs, and your table is complete.

UNPLUGGED
BY ASIA PIAŚCIK

Based in Warsaw, Poland, Asia Piaścik's one-man design studio Dingflux is notable for its diverse output. Attracted to multiple design disciplines, Asia constantly strives to involve himself in projects that cross the borders between product design and areas such as music, programming or architecture.

Concentrating on the relationships that develop between objects and their users, his design process aspires to create intriguing and unusual works that evoke a wide range of emotional responses. Conscious that this can be rooted in the effects created by proportion and scale, Asia makes cardboard models of his designs at a very early stage to gain a tactile experience of their look and feel in a way that is not possible with a drawing or computer rendering.

While our society becomes more reluctant to repair things and creates mountains of discarded objects and materials, Asia likes to give them a second chance, taking a little pressure off the environment. However, sometimes the choice of recycled materials is just a way of staying within a project's budget.

The Unplugged lamp is assembled in this spirit of recycling, combining spare bicycle parts and furniture to create a unique lamp that does not require a plug, but rather a little input from the user. It is, of course, also a tribute to the 'Readymades' of Marcel Duchamp, but one which upcycles a functional item into an art object.

www.dingflux.com

UNPLUGGED

MATERIALS
↑ High stool
↑ Bicycle fork (choose a fork with a screw thread on the steerer tube as it will be easier to install)
↑ 2 nuts
↑ Ready-made bicycle wheel with a dynamo drive hub (or a hub with dynamo drive, rim, spokes, spoke nipples)
↑ Inner tube
↑ Sand
↑ Adhesive tape
↑ Tyre
↑ Thin steel tube or rod to hold the light. Part of a motorcycle mirror has been used here, but any part can be substituted, as long as it is made of steel
↑ Glue or nuts and bolts
↑ Dynamo bicycle light
↑ Thin cable for electric connection
↑ Weight to stabilize (optional)

TOOLS
↑ Drill

Drill a central hole through the seat of the stool. It should be the diameter of the steerer tube of the bicycle fork. Most forks have a diameter of 2.5cm (1in) or 3cm (1⅛in).

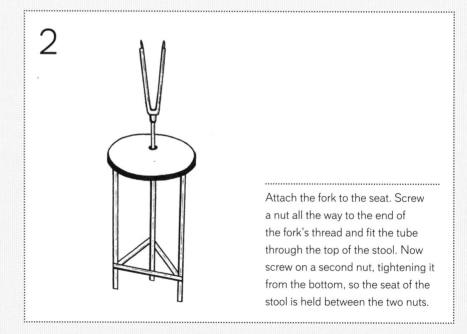

Attach the fork to the seat. Screw a nut all the way to the end of the fork's thread and fit the tube through the top of the stool. Now screw on a second nut, tightening it from the bottom, so the seat of the stool is held between the two nuts.

3

Prepare the wheel if not already assembled, inserting spokes into the rim and fitting the dynamo drive hub.

4

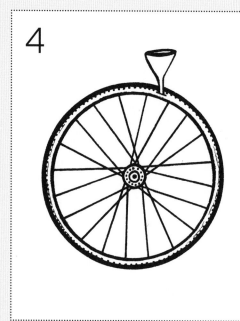

Cut open the inner tube and fill it with sand. This will make the wheel carry more momentum, improving the flywheel effect and extending the time the wheel spins. Reseal the tube with adhesive tape.

5

Fit the inner tube and tyre onto the wheel. Mount the wheel onto the bicycle fork.

6

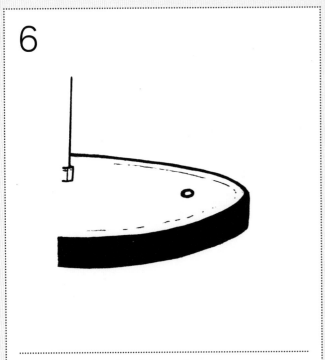

Drill a hole on the edge of the stool seat, the same diameter as the tube that will hold the light.

7

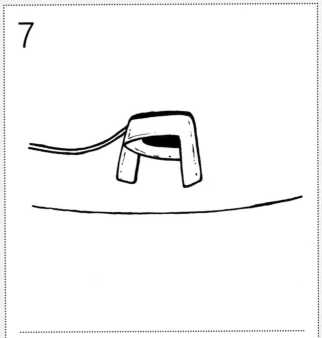

Fix the steel tube through the hole, securing it from below. This could be done in different ways, such as with glue or nuts and bolts, depending on what you are using for the tube.

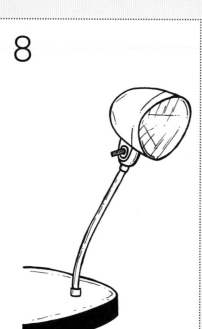

8

Mount the bicycle lamp at the top of the tube, preferably so that it is possible to tilt and adjust the angle of the light.

9

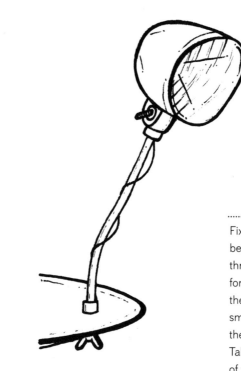

Fix the electrical connection between the hub and the light, threading the thin wire through the fork and into the mounting hole in the seat. If your fork does not have a small hole to thread through, wrap the wire around the fork instead. Take the wire across the bottom of the seat, through the other hole and wind it around the tube before connecting it to the light. Take care to complete the circuit, as the light will not work properly otherwise.

10

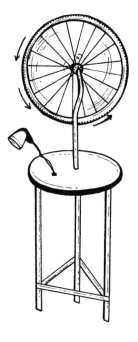

Spin the wheel, noting if the dynamo drive specifies a direction of rotation. If so, mark the direction clearly on the rim of the wheel.

11

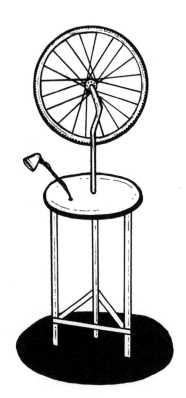

You might need to add weight to the base of the stool for stability. In this example, the stool is welded to a circular steel plate to keep it stable, especially during rotation. Suit the method to your particular stool.

COPPER-PIPE CLOTHING RAIL
BY MADELYNN FURLONG

Focusing on minimalist designs and drawing inspiration from the natural world, Madelynn Furlong aims to simplify, while bringing elements from the outside, inside. The Minneapolis-based designer prefers to work with recycled materials, believing that this plays an important part in taking care of the world we live in and enriching the life we lead. In reusing things, she also enjoys furthering the life and story of each particular item, and delights in the experiences and people she encounters through the making process. Madelynn aims to create pieces she knows will function and remain desirable for at least ten years.

The Copper-Pipe Clothing Rail is an easy-to-make project, combining copper pipes and natural cotton rope to create simple yet elegant storage for clothing and textiles — Madelynn is a firm believer that beautiful clothing should be displayed, rather than hidden away in dark wardrobes.

Used copper pipes can be found in scrapyards or in houses where heating or plumbing systems are being replaced. If you don't have a pipe cutter, any pieces you gather can be trimmed to length with a hacksaw before being cleaned up and polished if necessary. Failing that, all these components are available in DIY shops. This example uses standard 15mm (⅝in)-diameter pipe, but you could use 22mm (1in) for a more robust look.

COPPER-PIPE CLOTHING RAIL

The exact lengths of pipe are not critical, as long as you have three identical pairs of the same diameter.

MATERIALS
↑ 2 copper stop ends (pipe caps)
↑ 2 x 60cm (24in) copper pipes
↑ 2 x 40cm (15¾in) copper pipes
↑ 2 x 24cm (9½in) copper pipes
↑ 2 copper T-joints
↑ 2 copper elbow joints
↑ All-purpose cement glue
↑ 4mm (⅛in)-thick cotton rope, long enough to attach to your ceiling on either side of the rail
↑ 2 strong hooks

TOOLS
↑ Drill

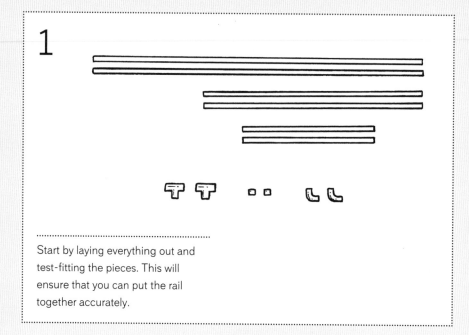

1

Start by laying everything out and test-fitting the pieces. This will ensure that you can put the rail together accurately.

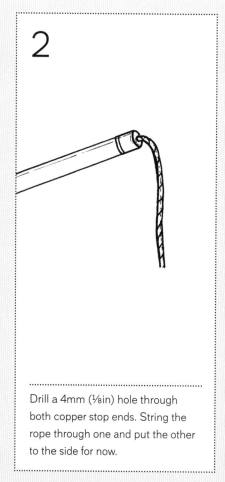

2

Drill a 4mm (⅛in) hole through both copper stop ends. String the rope through one and put the other to the side for now.

Attach the cap to the end of the first 40cm (15¾in) pipe and continue to string the rope through the pipe. Make sure to glue the copper pieces together as you go.

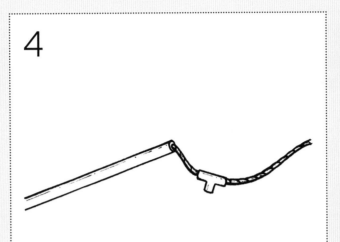

Attach a copper T-joint to the end, making sure the T faces inwards, and thread the rope through.

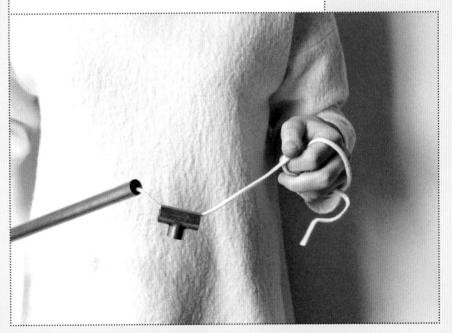

5

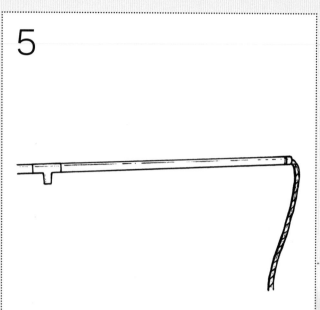

On the other end of the T add the 24cm (9½in) copper pipe.

6

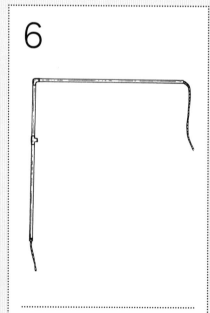

Now add the copper elbow and the first 60cm (24in) copper pipe, gluing and pulling the rope through as you go.

7

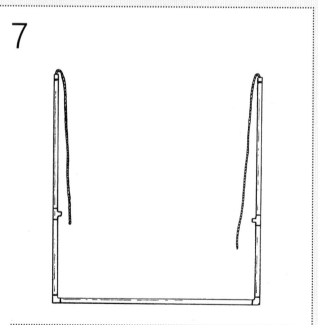

Work your way up the other side, starting with the elbow and ending with the second copper stop end, pulling the rope completely through.

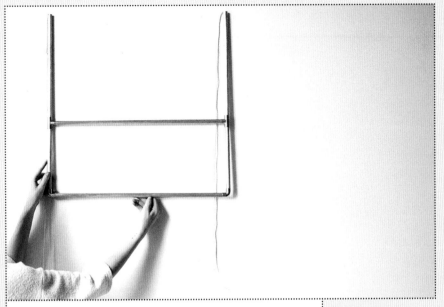

8

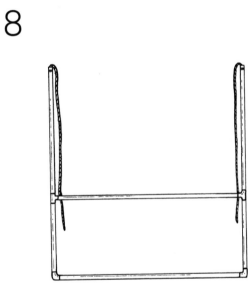

Once you have the outside frame complete, add the central 60cm (24in) pipe and glue together. This may require a bit of wiggling.

9

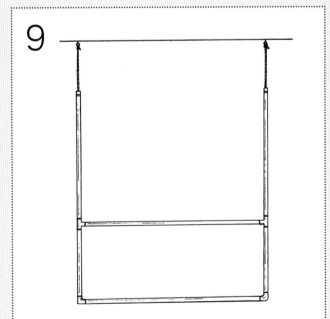

Attach the hooks securely to the ceiling, suspend your frame using the rope and then you're ready to start hanging your clothing.

PLASTIC BLOOMS
BY SARAH TURNER

Sarah Turner is an eco-artist and designer, specializing in making lighting, sculptures, artworks and decorative items from empty plastic bottles. All of her materials come from a network of donors made up of friends, family and strangers whom she calls her 'Bottle Army'. Sarah believes that people appreciate seeing that their rubbish is being used for something fun, rather than harming the environment.

The bottles are cleaned and sandblasted, which turns the transparent plastic to a frosted white and allows it to be dyed with vibrant colours. Then, with intricate cutting and sculpting, the bottles are transformed into new products that give little clue to their origins. After all, as Sarah declares, 'just because a product is made from rubbish, it doesn't mean it needs to look like it!' Following a more conventional design process, a designer can simply choose the material best suited to a product; with upcycling, the designer is stuck with a material and forced to work within its limitations. However, Sarah appreciates this challenge because it forces her to explore and take advantage of a material's properties and it inspires her to use them in new ways.

The Plastic Blooms project is perfectly suited to the qualities of plastic bottles. They can be a little fiddly to begin with, but once you have learnt the techniques they are quite straightforward and fun to make. You can even design a unique flower by experimenting with different designs, petal shapes, patterns and configurations.

www.sarahturner.co.uk

PLASTIC BLOOMS

MATERIALS
↑ Plastic bottles
↑ Card
↑ Stainless steel or aluminium rod
↑ Insulation tape
↑ Coloured tape (optional)
↑ Nail polish or permanent
   markers (optional)

TOOLS
↑ Craft knife
↑ Leather punch

Gather a selection of empty plastic bottles. Different shades of the same colour work well.

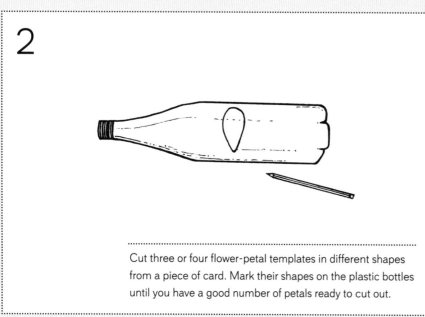

Cut three or four flower-petal templates in different shapes from a piece of card. Mark their shapes on the plastic bottles until you have a good number of petals ready to cut out.

3

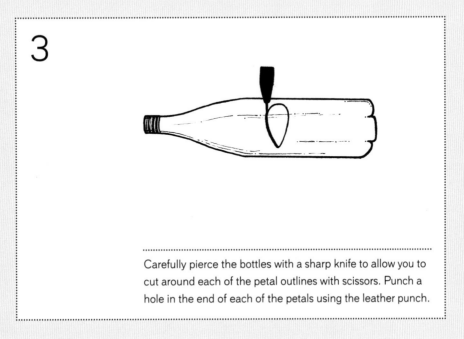

Carefully pierce the bottles with a sharp knife to allow you to cut around each of the petal outlines with scissors. Punch a hole in the end of each of the petals using the leather punch.

4

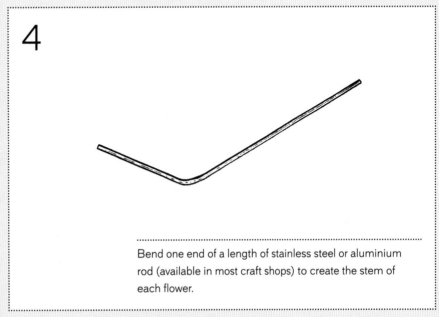

Bend one end of a length of stainless steel or aluminium rod (available in most craft shops) to create the stem of each flower.

5

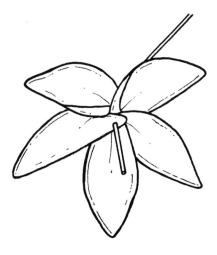

Thread each of the petals onto the stem, spacing them evenly.

6

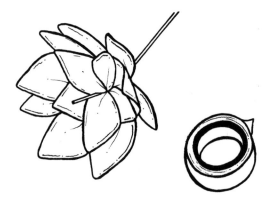

Cut a short piece of electrical insulation tape into thin lengths. Wrap a strip around the stem in front of the flower and a strip behind to keep it in place. If you like, you can cover this with coloured tape to match your petals.

7

Create a bouquet using a variety of petal shapes and styles. You can add a small disk of plastic in the centre of each bloom, if liked. For further decoration you can create patterns on the petals using nail polish or permanent markers.

CROSS-STITCH CHAIR
BY CINTIA GONZALEZ

Cintia Gonzalez describes her work as creating something useful and beautiful out of things that were previously unloved. She publishes her own weekly DIY craft projects, aimed at readers of all skill levels, on her My Poppet blog, hoping to encourage and inspire readers to be creative and resourceful. She also sells her own pieces in the webshop of the same name.

Preferring to use second-hand or vintage items, Cintia finds inspiration in her extensive collection of vintage fabrics and garments, relishing the idea that objects all have a history, even if it is unknown to us. She hates waste, too, and challenges herself to create things with even the tiniest scraps.

Gleaning most of her supplies from charity shops or flea markets, and drawing on her skills in crochet, sewing, needle felting, papercraft and quilting, Cintia explores the fine line between an object's utility or desirability and obsolescence.

The Cross-Stitch Chair is a perfect illustration of this distinction, using minimal materials to give new life to a handwoven cane seat that was found abandoned by the roadside. Cintia spent three days sewing the colourful panels and, although the chair was a little weathered, a light sanding and a coat of Danish oil left it ready for a new existence. Try replicating her pattern on your own piece of cane furniture.

mypoppet.com.au

CROSS-STITCH CHAIR

MATERIALS
↑ Cane chair
↑ Danish oil
↑ Wool or silk embroidery thread in several different colours

TOOLS
↑ Fine sandpaper
↑ Embroidery needle

1

Find an old piece of cane furniture. A stool would work just as well as a dining chair. Pressed and handwoven cane seats both feature the sort of intricate patterns that can be embroidered.

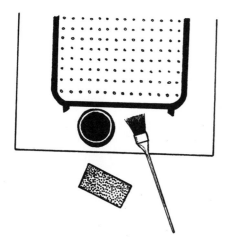

2

Give the wooden frame a light sand with fine sandpaper, then a light coat of Danish oil. Danish oil is a good alternative to varnish as it conditions the wood and gives a satin finish, as well as bringing out the wood's natural colour.

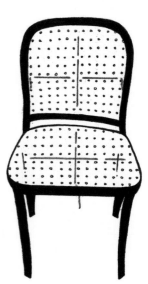

3

Thread your needle and use it to mark out the centre line of the weave in both directions on both the seat and back of the chair.

4

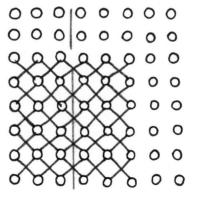

Using a cross stitch, sew a square of 5 x 5 stitches in the centre. The cross-stitch technique is exactly the same as you would use for a tapestry canvas, but try to keep the back of the stitching as tidy as possible. Don't use any knots to fasten the yarn as they will be visible — just let the stitching itself hold the loose ends securely.

5

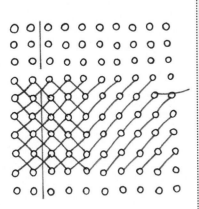

Changing the colour of your yarn, continue to work outwards, stitching 5 x 5 squares in different colour blocks.

6

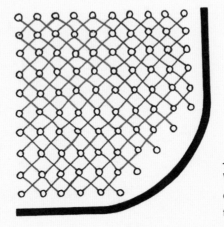

When you reach the edge of your cane area, simply sew as much of the block as possible before you meet the wood. Mix up the design with triangles and other geometric shapes to make your pattern unique.

F.AID
BY MISCHER'
TRAXLER STUDIO

Mischer'Traxler Studio is the Vienna-based partnership of Katharina Mischer and Thomas Traxler. The duo see design as a very wide field and are involved in works ranging from products to production processes, as well as installations and interactive projects. Creating their projects as a means of communication, Mischer'Traxler's goal is to show that design can be good, functional and beautiful — not just the object itself, but also the idea that it stands for.

As a demonstration of this, Mischer'Traxler make frequent use of recycled materials. Their attraction is not just that they are easy to come by, cheap and often good quality, but they also highlight the potential and value in materials which can be repurposed rather than thrown away.

F.aid is Mischer'Traxler's DIY method of creating furniture from waste fibreboard pieces, fixing them together with bandages. The bandages (intended for lightweight medical casts) harden quickly on contact with water, giving stability to the furniture as well as an unconventional look.

The duo's f.aid workshops allow participants to build their own furniture, creating shelves, lamps and seating using this simple method. The project makes use of non-recyclable chipboard, MDF and other fibreboards, which would otherwise be destroyed in high-temperature incineration plants. Every year, 2.5 million cubic metres (88 million cubic feet) of these materials are produced in Austria and they are very difficult to recycle.

www.mischertraxler.com

F.AID

MATERIALS
↑ Scrap wood such as chipboard, MDF or other fibreboards
↑ Screws or nails
↑ 3M Scotchcast plaster bandages
↑ Acetone (optional)
↑ Paint (optional)

TOOLS
↑ Drill, screwdriver or hammer
↑ Rubber gloves
↑ Brush

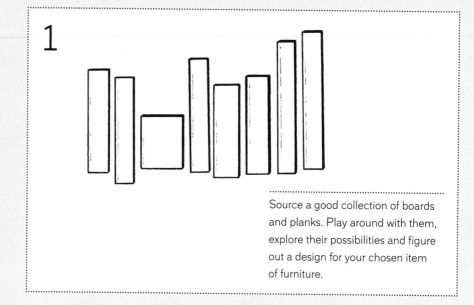

1

Source a good collection of boards and planks. Play around with them, explore their possibilities and figure out a design for your chosen item of furniture.

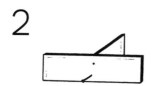

2

Fix the boards roughly into position with screws or nails. Don't worry about neatness, as the joints will be hidden later.

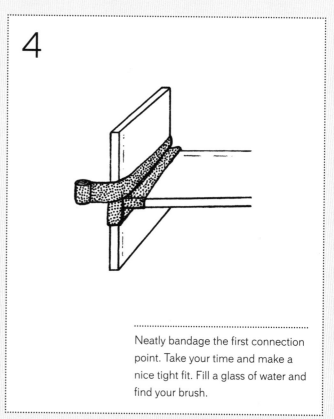

4

Neatly bandage the first connection point. Take your time and make a nice tight fit. Fill a glass of water and find your brush.

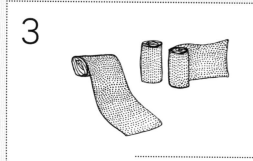

3

Take the bandages out of their packaging. Don't unpack them too early as the bandages will dry out slightly in the air. It is a good idea to wear gloves, as the bandages become quite sticky.

5

Hold the end of the bandage in position and use the wet brush to dampen the whole connection. Don't use too much water, but try to work the brush with a bit of pressure. Continue bandaging the connection points until your piece is complete.

6

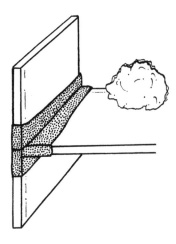

Wait around 20 minutes before cleaning any stains from the board with a wet cloth. If necessary you may need to use acetone. Try painting the bandages in contrasting colours, if you like.

WOODEN WALL SCULPTURE
BY MARTIN GERSTENBERGER

Combining design work with painting, drawing and sculpture, Martin Gerstenberger believes in taking a playful approach and experimenting as much as possible. Working in a number of disciplines also means he is able to switch to a new field if lacking good ideas in another, allowing the flow of work to continue uninterrupted.

Rather than fulfil any master plan or follow a strict theoretical idea, the German designer simply aims to channel his reserve of Art Brut/Outsider Art energy, doing whatever comes into his mind. Sometimes this leads to surprising results that he is unable to explain. Generally speaking, however, whether painting or building, he favours a clear, minimalist design and a relatively simple composition.

Martin's primary reason for using recycled materials in his work is an appreciation of the patina of age, which cannot be imitated. He is also entertained by the idea that items such as shields and metal buckets have fulfilled their first role in life and now have a chance to become something completely new. When such cheap and useful items are easy to find, he feels there is no need to consider new materials. And as this also helps to avoid a little bit of waste, then so much the better.

The toy building blocks used for this project are given the opportunity to enjoy a new life in a more sedate capacity, out of the reach of tiny hands. However, Martin suggests would-be builders think back to playing with blocks like these as children themselves, in order to rediscover that carefree playfulness.

martingerstenberger.weebly.com

WOODEN WALL SCULPTURE

MATERIALS
↑ Scrap wood or toy building
  blocks
↑ Acrylic paint
↑ Wall-mounting plate
↑ Wood glue
↑ Varnish

TOOLS
↑ Drill and screws
↑ Clamps or elastic bands

1

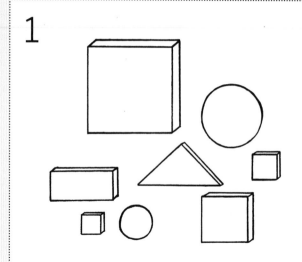

Gather your materials. The sculpture can be made from different-shaped pieces of scrap timber cut to size, although a simpler approach is to use toy building blocks. Using round or triangular components as well as square and oblong shapes will make the sculpture more interesting.

2

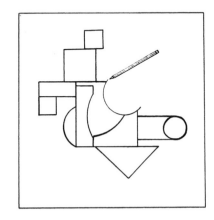

Draw a rough sketch of the desired form or simply lay the pieces down on a table and arrange them into a design. Spread the pieces evenly, ensuring the sculpture does not have too much weight on one side. A large piece should be used in the centre for affixing the wall-mounting plate to. Once you have created the form of your sculpture take a photo, so that you can remove the parts for painting and then return them to the correct positions.

3

Choose a colour scheme and paint the wood pieces. Using a range of lighter and darker tones will emphasize the different shapes and relief, particularly if the front of each piece is bright and the other surfaces are painted neutrally. Fasten the wall-mounting plate to the weight-bearing central piece using a drill and appropriate fixings.

4

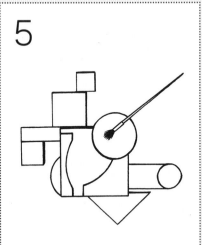

Glue the pieces into position, referring to your photograph if necessary. Start from the middle, working towards one edge, then return to the middle and complete the other side. Finish the whole width of the sculpture before adding any extra pieces on top. To make sure the sculpture is securely glued, it can be held together at this stage using clamps or elastic bands.

5

Varnish the finished sculpture to increase the brightness of the colours and protect it against dust.

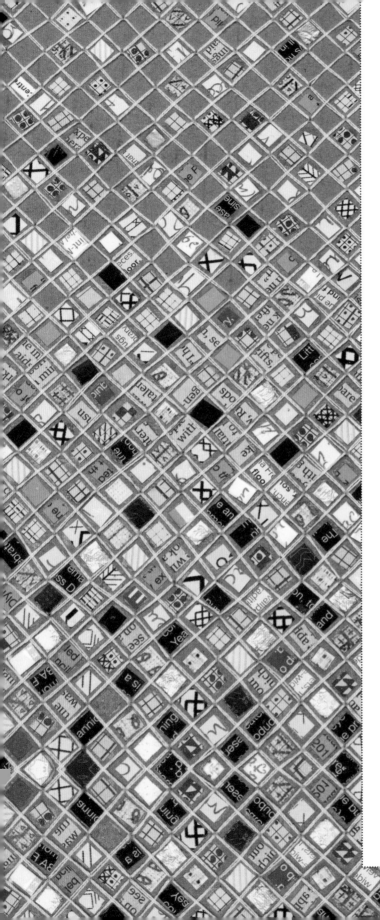

PIXELATE
BY RACHEL PARKER

Rachel Parker is a British freelance textile designer, producing work for Flock, a design studio that works with emerging designers to create interior fabrics with a focus on colour and geometric design. Rachel also sells original handstitched artworks in her webshop, Pixel&Thread. This name neatly captures the nature of her work, which unites traditional embroidery techniques with contemporary digital design — an approach Rachel likes to call 'digital craft'.

Learning to cross stitch was Rachel's first experience with textiles and has remained a constant inspiration, complementing her love of grids, repetition and geometric shapes. Cross stitching is also an extremely versatile way of decorating a host of recycled materials, from book pages to drilled wooden tabletops, as well as scraps of fabric.

Crafting is also a way for Rachel to reuse the scraps of paper she likes to collect, such as the insides of envelopes, old shopping lists or glossy magazines. She finds that giving a new identity to the textures and patterns in discarded everyday items is a satisfying way to create something unexpected and beautiful.

Pixelate employs similar discarded materials to create a handstitched collage artwork. It's a project that uses materials found around the house and works with many different combinations of papers and colour. This example uses photographs, sweet (candy) wrappers, newspaper, magazine and book pages, a handwritten letter, postcards, envelopes and vintage embroidery patterns. The base material came from a cardboard box.

www.rachelparkerdesigns.co.uk

PIXELATE

MATERIALS
↿ Graph paper
↿ Corrugated cardboard,
   23 x 23cm (9 x 9in)
↿ Masking tape
↿ Embroidery cotton (floss)
↿ Assortment of interesting
   collage papers — book pages,
   magazines, photos, etc.

TOOLS
↿ Sharp needle
↿ Craft knife
↿ Cutting mat
↿ PVA glue
↿ Cocktail stick (optional)

1

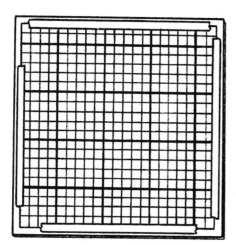

Trim the graph paper, making it 2cm (¾in) smaller than
the corrugated cardboard all around. Lightly tape it to the
back of the cardboard, making sure it is central. Low-tack
masking tape will mean the paper is less likely to rip when
the tape is peeled off later.

2

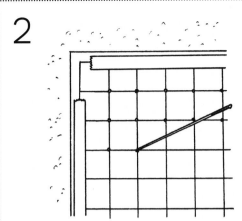

Use a sharp needle to punch holes through both the graph paper and the cardboard at 1cm (⅜in) intervals, using the graph paper as a guide. It helps to lay some felt or chunky fabric on the table and work on top of this, keeping the surface flat. Flip the paper over to make sure no holes have been missed, then carefully remove the masking tape.

3

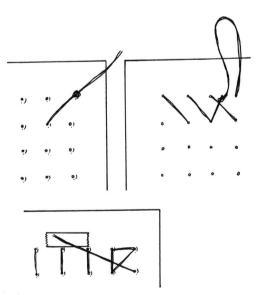

Cut a long strand of embroidery cotton, fold it in half and thread the folded end through the needle, leaving the loop at the end. Pass the needle through from the back of the cardboard to the front, then reinsert it back through the cardboard, one hole down and to the right, to make the first diagonal stitch. On the back of the cardboard, secure the thread by passing the needle through the loop of thread left previously.

Cross stitch onto the cardboard through the holes, working in horizontal rows. When the cotton runs out, simply thread it through some of the stitches on the reverse to hold it in place, trim and secure with a small piece of masking tape.

4

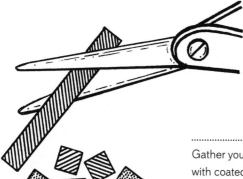

Gather your papers and sort them into piles. Play around with coated, textured and patterned papers to get different effects. Fragments of text also make interesting collage materials. Take the chosen papers and slice them into strips approximately 5mm (¼in) wide using a craft knife and cutting mat, then take these strips and chop them into little squares — they don't need to be perfect!

5

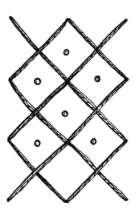

Starting at the bottom corner and working in small sections, dab a small dot of PVA glue into each diamond-shaped space between the stitches. Be sparing, a little goes a long way. Applying the glue using a cocktail stick helps.

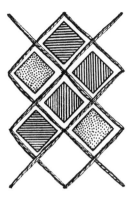

6

Carefully place one paper square on top of each drop of glue, keeping a generally even distribution of different patterns and papers. Create a pixelated effect by concentrating the bulk of the collage at the base of the design and leaving more gaps towards the top. Continue until the collage is complete. Allow to dry before framing, if wished.

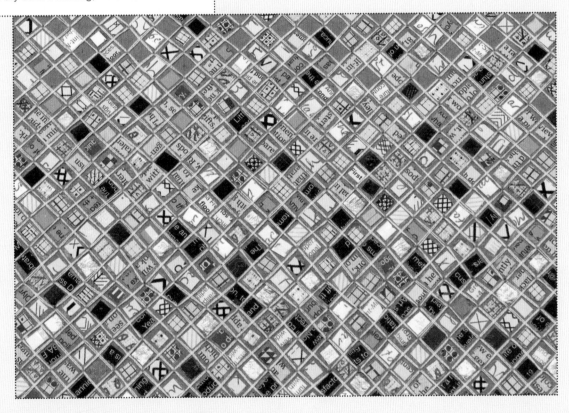

PALLET WINDOW SHELF
BY CHRISTOPHER BERRY

Based in rural England at the foot of the South Downs, Factorytwentyone is a home-accessories company aiming to create affordable, eco-friendly household products. Founded by Christopher Berry, the company's range includes lampshades made from recycled wooden pallets, as well as coat hooks and iPhone holders made from oak.

Christopher divides his time between Factorytwentyone and working with his father, creating medieval-style furniture and architectural woodwork. This large-scale work provides him with much of the material he uses for his own designs, happily chiming with his preference for using recycled timber. Much of his work comes from scraps of oak beams, which are too small to be made into furniture but are perfectly suited for shaping into handy organizers for the home.

His other source of material is wooden pallets, discarded and left to rot on industrial estates. Conscious that wood is wasted on a grand scale, the designer considers any recycling efforts that benefit the environment are worthwhile, no matter how small. Another advantage of recycling is the abundance of low-cost or free materials and being able to pass these savings on to the customer.

The Pallet Window Shelf project was created especially for this book and neatly encapsulates Christopher's preference for simple and original designs, crafted from recycled wood with a mix of traditional manufacturing techniques and modern processes. This is a pretty easy project, requiring only a few basic tools, although Christopher points out that it is worth taking the time to ensure the holes are lined up neatly.

www.factorytwentyone.co.uk

PALLET WINDOW SHELF

MATERIALS
↑ Wooden pallet
↑ Strong string or cord

TOOLS
↑ Crowbar
↑ Hammer
↑ Large flat-head screwdriver
↑ Saw
↑ Pliers
↑ Plane and vice (optional)
↑ Drill

1

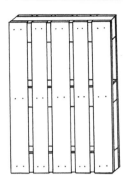

Find a wooden pallet in good condition. Consider the width of the boards — wide will make a deep shelf, and thin a narrow shelf. Now break the pallet apart. This is often quite difficult and calls for a determined approach, using a crowbar, hammer and large screwdriver to prise it apart. Alternatively, saw the boards if you don't mind losing a bit of length. Once dismantled, remove the nails using pliers or the claw end of the hammer.

2

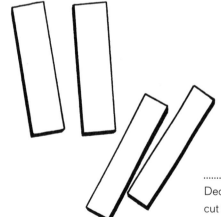

Decide on the size of your window shelf, then measure and cut the boards to their required length with the saw. If you are after a rustic look, leave the edges as they are. If you'd prefer the window shelf to have a new and modern look, plane the edges smooth, clamping the boards in a vice or work bench.

3

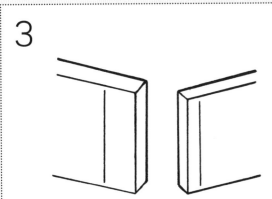

Test fit the window frame together to check the size and ensure all the measurements are correct. Make any necessary adjustments. Lay the boards out to form a neat L-shape, where the end of one plank butts up against the side of the next. Now draw a line on the inside of the corner so one plank has a marked area equal to the thickness of the other plank. On the other plank, draw a line across the end, 1cm (⅜in) in from the edge.

4

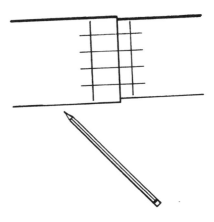

Now lay the planks flat, end to end, with the marked ends against each other. Draw 4 or 5 small lines between the marks running parallel to the length of the boards. These marks will indicate where to drill holes for string to run through. Repeat this for the other 3 corners of the shelf.

5

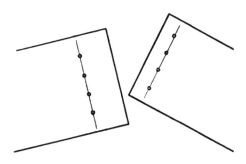

Choose a drill bit large enough to make a hole that the string can pass through easily. Drill through all the boards at the points where the parallel lines meet the other marks.

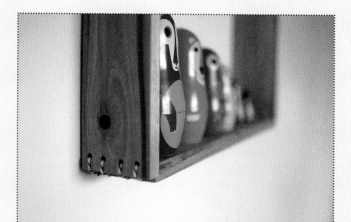

6

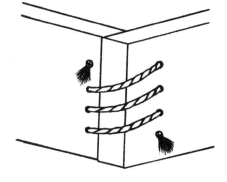

Feed the string through the holes, pulling the boards neatly together. Repeat this at the other corners. Just like lacing up a shoe, it is possible to use different types of stitching.

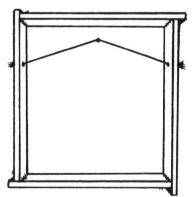

7

Drill a hole in the side of each frame near the top and back of the uprights. Thread another piece of string through these holes and tie a knot at each end. It is now ready to be hung and displayed.

WINE-BOX OTTOMAN
BY CHLOE EDWARDS

Chloe Edwards' company Made Anew produces upcycled furniture and accessories, changing the original intention of objects to create contemporary designs for the home and the body. Often exploring a theme of everyday decadence, her eclectic range of designs extends from chandelier jewellery to wine-box ottomans.

The streets surrounding Chloe's East London studio are full of what she calls 'street treasure', and her inspiration to upcycle comes from her ability to see possibilities in abandoned items. From battered chairs to old steamer trunks and even the odd table, she rejoices in taking discarded objects that come with their own story and reinventing them to add a whole new chapter. Chloe's previous home was filled almost entirely with furniture made from street treasure — a wonderful jumble of past and present reinvention.

The Wine-Box Ottoman is intended to offer multifunctional storage, to help make the most of small city dwellings, or to provide a centrepiece for larger homes. It can be used as a footstool, storage box or even a makeshift table.

The design allows some variation in materials. It can be made with wine boxes or apple crates, and the fabric can be anything at all — Chloe has been commissioned to upholster boxes with old curtain fabric, blankets and even a tweed coat.

www.madeanew.co.uk

WINE-BOX OTTOMAN

MATERIALS
- ↖ Wooden wine box/crate, 12-bottle size
- ↖ Wood wax
- ↖ 9mm (⅜in) wooden lid, cut to fit your box
- ↖ 50mm (2in) double-sided tape
- ↖ 25mm (1in) medium-density upholstery foam, cut to fit your lid
- ↖ Cotton wadding (batting), the length of your lid plus 20cm (8in)
- ↖ Thick fabric to upholster the lid, the size of the lid plus 10cm (4in) all around
- ↖ Contrasting lighter-weight fabric for the underside of the lid, about 5cm (2in) smaller all around (enough to cover the stapled fabric)
- ↖ 2mm (1/12in) card, slightly smaller than the lighter fabric
- ↖ 2 small brass hinges
- ↖ Screws shorter than the thickness of your box (use snips to cut off any excess, if needed)
- ↖ 30cm (11¾in) chandelier chain or cotton webbing, cut into two equal lengths
- ↖ 8 upholstery tacks (brass or silver)

TOOLS
- ↖ Medium sandpaper
- ↖ Staple gun
- ↖ Drill with small bit
- ↖ Hammer

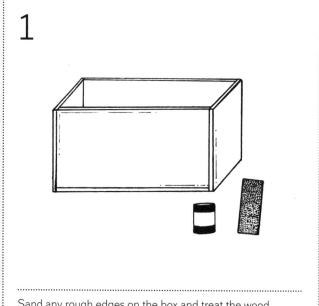

1

Sand any rough edges on the box and treat the wood with wax inside and out, following the manufacturer's instructions. Try to avoid waxing the top edge where the lid will sit, as this may mark your fabric. Give this edge a light sanding after waxing to make sure it is clean.

2

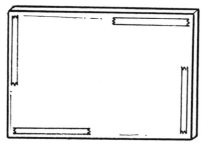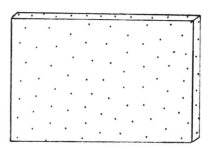

Lightly sand the edges and corners of your wooden lid. Apply a few strips of double-sided tape to one side of the lid, then stick the foam neatly on top. The tape will hold it in place during upholstering.

3

Lay the cotton wadding on a flat surface. Position the lid on top, foam side down, so that there is an extra 10cm (4in) of wadding at each end. Fold the overlapping wadding ends over and staple them to the wooden side of the lid. Start by stapling the centre of one side, then pull the wadding taut and staple it at the centre of the opposite side. Continue moving out equally on either side until all is stapled. This will give a firm, smooth finish to your lightly cushioned lid.

4

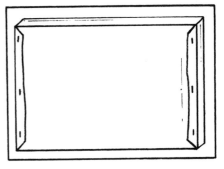

Iron the thick fabric. Lay it on a flat surface, wrong side up. Place the wood/foam/batting sandwich centrally on the fabric, leaving an equal excess of material on all sides.

5

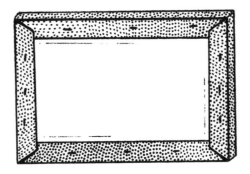

Repeat the stapling process as described in Step 3, working from the centre outwards, but rather than stapling to the ends, leave about a 7cm (2¾in) gap on each side to allow for folding the fabric inside. Pull the fabric taut, making sure any patterns or lines are centred and straight. Tuck the excess material in neatly at each end (on the short side), making sure the fabric is taut before stapling to secure.

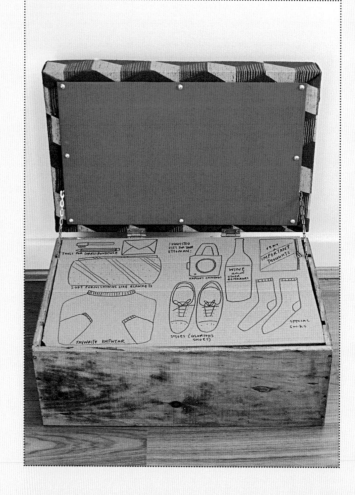

Prepare the inner-lid cover. Iron the lighter-weight fabric. Place the thick card in the centre with an equal excess of fabric all round. Stick double-sided tape along each edge of the card, then neatly wrap the fabric edges over to secure, starting with the opposite long edges, then the shorter edges, tucking in the corners again. The front side of the card should be covered by smooth fabric. Set aside.

7

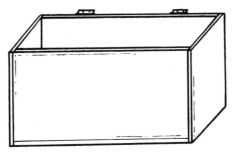

Decide which of the long sides of the box is the front. On the opposite side, make a pencil mark 10cm (4in) in from each end. Hold a hinge in place on the top edge of the box against this measurement and make circular marks through the screw holes. Repeat at the other end and drill 2mm (1/12in) holes through the marks. Screw on the hinges, making sure they open outwards.

8

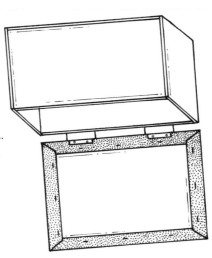

Place the box on its side on a flat surface with the hinges at the bottom. Now place the lid, fabric side down, in position to attach it to the hinges. You may need to put a couple of books or magazines under the box to bring it to the same level as the lid. To ensure the lid is fitted centrally, line it up against the box and mark the position of the hinges. Slide the lid back a little until it is aligned with the flat part of the hinge and mark the position of the holes.

Tip: Only drill one hole and fix each hinge with a single screw first, in case minor adjustments need to be made to the alignment. Drill the remaining holes and screw the hinges together.

9

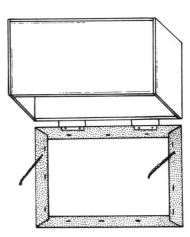

Keeping the box on its side, position the inner lid cover, noting where it needs to sit to cover the stapled areas. Drill a pilot hole then screw one end of the chain to the wooden inner lid about 8cm (3in) in from the hinged edge and 2cm (¾in) in from the short side edge. Repeat on the other side.

10

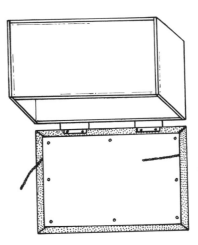

Reinsert the inner lid cover, covering the screws and any area not upholstered. Secure the cover with upholstery tacks, tapping them in with a hammer, placing one at each corner and one at the centre of each edge.

11

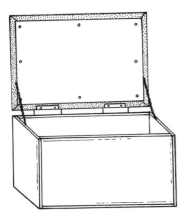

To secure the other end of the chain, sit the box the right way up and hold the lid open far enough back that it will not fall shut. Pull the chain taut, creating an equal-sided triangle between chain, box and lid, then mark the position of the chain inside the box, 2cm (¾in) in from the edge. Drill a pilot hole then fix the end of the chain with a screw. Repeat on the other side.

RAG RUG
BY ANGELA WEISSENFELS

Angela Weissenfels felt compelled to start upcycling in response to the sheer amount of waste people produce, as well as the abundance of useful but unwanted materials in her own home. In particular, the German designer began to realize the potential of her own outdated clothes and old sheets. Rather than throw these away, Angela decided to set up Made by Noir to experiment with these and other unwanted items, and create decorations and usable art.

Although her company has only been established for a short time, Angela has already created designs from a wide range of discarded materials, from wood and concrete, to paper, plastic and metal cans. She has also started to make use of the large number of glass jars she has collected from storing spices and preserves, turning them into table lights and vases, and has begun experimenting with plaster and recycled fabric to create decorative art. Her latest designs are a response to the huge number of plastic bags thrown away every day — she is searching for creative ways to upcycle these bags into something useful so as to keep them out of landfill.

This project uses unwanted textiles such as duvet covers, pillowcases, curtains, sheets and clothing to create a rustic-looking rug. Cotton works very well, but you can use whatever fabric you have available.

www.etsy.com/uk/shop/MadebyNoir

RAG RUG

MATERIALS
↑ Old cotton textiles

TOOLS
↑ Fabric scissors
↑ Crochet hook, 12 or 15mm
   (O/16 or P/19)
↑ Needle and thread

These instructions use the UK term
'double crochet' (dc) — equivalent to the
US 'single crochet' (sc).

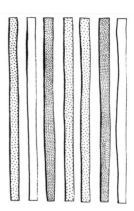

1

Cut the fabric into roughly 3cm (1in)-wide strips. This measurement is a guide; experiment with various widths to see what suits you best — the width will depend on the fabric being used. To avoid having to cut every strip individually, start with a cut of about 5cm (2in) and then rip along the line. It doesn't matter if the strips are uneven or if the edges are frayed — these won't be visible in the end.

2

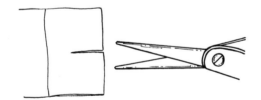

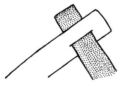

Once you have a large collection of strips, use them to create yarn. The easiest method is to cut a small slit in the ends of each strip and slipknot them together: thread a strip through the slit in another and then feed the tail of the first strip through the slit in its own end. Pull together tight and the strips should be connected.

3

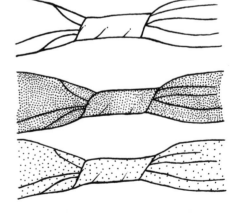

Do this with all the strips, bearing in mind the distribution of colours. It is possible to create various colour gradients and patterns at this stage.

4

Now crochet your rag rug in rounds following the instructions below.

Chain stitch 4 (5 for heavy material), slip stitch into the first chain to form a loop.
Row 1: Chain 1 (counts as first dc), 7 dc into loop
Row 2: 2 dc in each st (stitch)
Row 3: *2 dc in first st, 1 dc in next st (*repeat 7 times)
Row 4: *2 dc in first st, 1 dc in next st, 1 dc in next st (*repeat 7 times)

Continue increasing 1 dc in next stitch until the rug is as big as you want it.

5

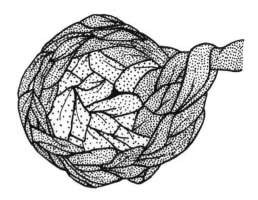

Ideally, the crochet rag rug should lie flat, but if it starts to buckle a bit, put a decrease in the row. Angela would opt to eliminate some of the 2 dc and 1 dc in them.

6

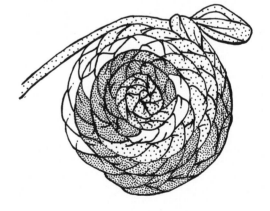

Once the rug is the desired size, or you have run out of material, secure the end of the yarn with a last chain stitch. Sew this end onto the rug to secure using a needle and thread.

STAR CUSHION
BY PLACE DE BLEU

Place de Bleu was founded in Copenhagen in 2010 with the purpose of creating jobs and a better future for marginalized immigrant women in Denmark. Many of these women are skilled but have failed to find work due to language difficulties, illness or lack of formal qualifications. This non-profit organization also helps to keep traditional craftsmanship alive, providing an outlet for workers from diverse backgrounds whose sewing, knitting and crocheting techniques have been inherited through generations.

Place de Bleu's geometric designs for home interiors and accessories are inspired by traditional patchwork, but strive to combine a contemporary Scandinavian aesthetic with the inspirations and influences of their diverse global workforce.

The company uses high-quality surplus material from the Danish textile manufacturer Kvadrat, ensuring durable products and a reduced impact on the environment. With their desire to emphasize quality craftsmanship, social responsibility and longevity in design, Place de Bleu subscribe to the 'Buy less, buy better' philosophy.

The Star Cushion is Place de Bleu's signature design, and aims to infuse a classic Moroccan cushion with a playful, modern Scandinavian feel. These instructions are for a cushion in two contrasting colours, although it can be made in a variety of colour and texture combinations.

www.placedebleu.dk

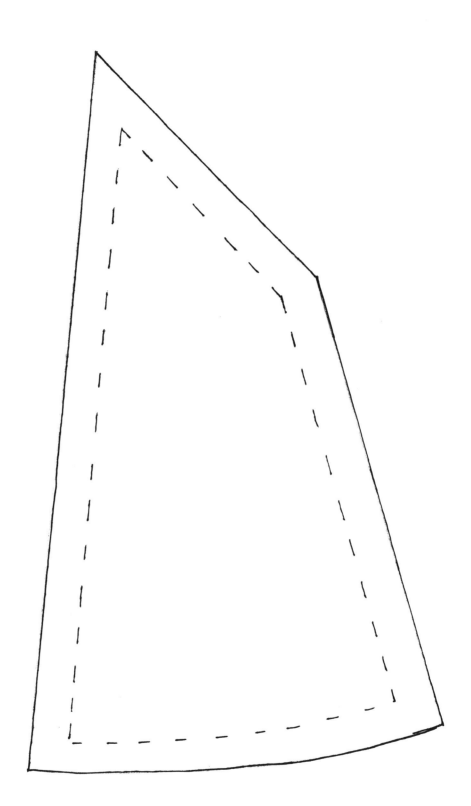

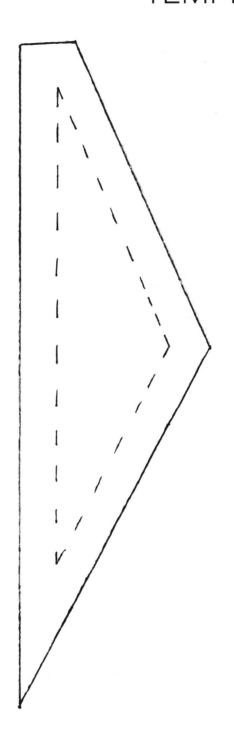

STAR CUSHION

MATERIALS
↑ Cardboard
↑ Approximately 50cm (19½in) of two discarded fabrics in different colours (suede and canvas were used here)
↑ Cushion pad, 45cm (17¾in) diameter
↑ Button

TOOLS
↑ Fabric pencil
↑ Fabric scissors or rotary cutter
↑ Pins, needle and thread

All measurements include 1cm (⅜in) seam allowances. Sew right sides together. The finished cushion has a diameter of 45cm (17¾in).

1

Using cardboard, make templates of the pattern pieces and use them to mark the shapes on your fabric with the pencil. Mark 8 small triangles (4 in each colour) and 8 four-sided shapes (4 in each colour). Now flip the templates over and repeat, creating another 8 small triangles (4 in each colour) and 8 four-sided shapes (4 in each colour).

2

Cut out all the marked shapes, then cut 2 half-circles with a diameter of 47cm (18½in) for the back in one of your colours.

3

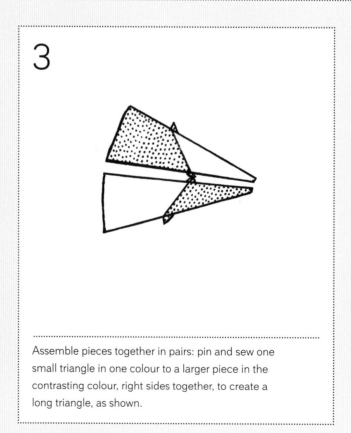

Assemble pieces together in pairs: pin and sew one small triangle in one colour to a larger piece in the contrasting colour, right sides together, to create a long triangle, as shown.

4

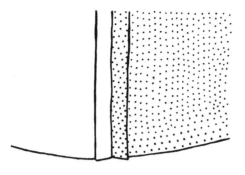

After stitching each piece, seams can either be pressed open, or to one side. Choose one method and stay consistent throughout. This reduces bulk and helps create a smoother finish. Repeat Steps 3 and 4 until you have 16 long triangle units.

5

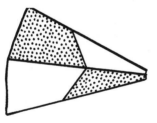

Sew 2 long triangles together, as shown. Repeat to make 8 triangle units in all.

6

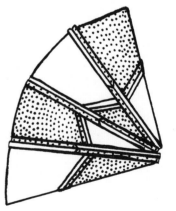

Sew 2 of these larger triangles together. Repeat to make 4 triangle units in all.

7

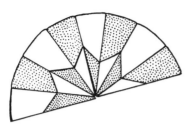

Sew 2 of the wider triangle units together. Now you should have 2 patchwork half-circles.

8

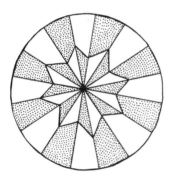

Sew these half-circles together to make one big star.

9

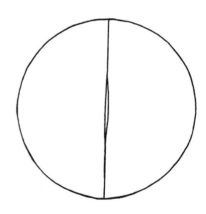

Sew together the 2 half-circles for the back, from the edge to the centre, leaving a 20cm (8in) gap in the centre. Press the seams.

11

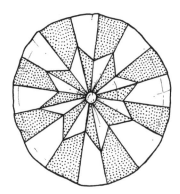

Handstitch a matching button in the centre of the star on the front.

10

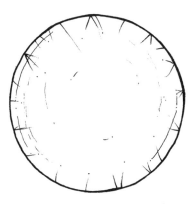

Sew together the front and back of the cushion. Turn the cushion right way out, insert the cushion pad and then handstitch the opening closed.

BOTTLE VASE
BY STELLA MELGRATI

Founded on a love of natural yarns and fabrics — wool, cotton, hemp and linen — Stella Melgrati's company, the Yarn Kitchen, celebrates these simple materials in all their forms. Currently based in Ferrara in the north of Italy, Stella takes an experimental approach to her work, playing with balls of yarn and waiting for new design ideas to occur. In her words, 'It's like speaking with the material and getting an unexpected answer each time.'

Stella cites two main reasons for using recycled materials in her work. The first is an appreciation of the finite nature of her resources and a desire to get the longest possible use from them. The other is her habit of collecting objects such as bottles, glass jars, plates, pebbles from the seashore, acorns and leaves. The beauty of these found objects provides Stella with an abundant source of inspiration. Playing around with these objects at home she finds that sometimes 'an object talks to me and asks for a new life … a milk bottle pretends to become a cool vase, a stripy sock pretends to become a rabbit.'

This project uses a milk bottle covered with chunky cotton rope in two contrasting colours to create a crocheted vase. Inspired by crocheted bottle covers popular in the 1960s, the design combines simple materials to celebrate an everyday object. Although this project is quite easy, crocheting with a cotton rope is a little more difficult than using cotton yarn. It gives a wonderful texture, though, so don't be put off!

www.etsy.com/uk/shop/theYarnKitchen

BOTTLE VASE

MATERIALS
↑ Cotton rope in two colours
↑ Glass milk bottle

TOOLS
↑ Medium crochet hook
↑ Small crochet hook

These instructions use the UK term 'double crochet' (dc) — equivalent to the US 'single crochet' (sc).

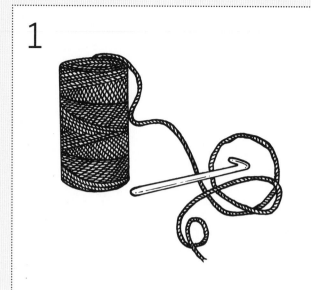

1

Row 1: Using a medium crochet hook and cotton rope, form a magic loop and work 7 dc in it. Mark the last dc because you will work in the round, so no end of a row will be detectable.

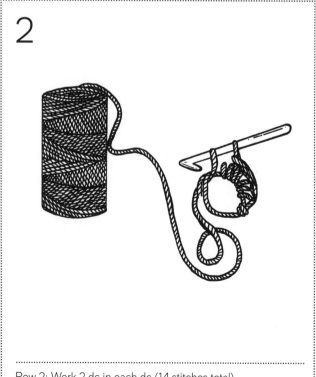

2

Row 2: Work 2 dc in each dc (14 stitches total).

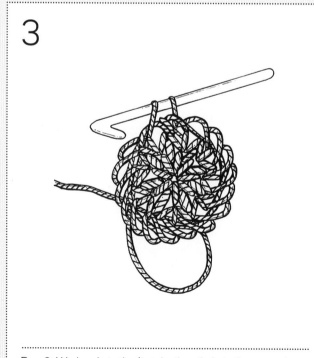

3

Row 3: Work a dc in the first dc, then 2 dc in the same dc until the end (27 stitches total).

4

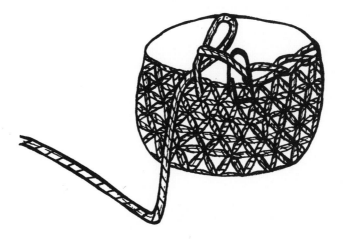

Continue working in the round, marking the last dc of the row each time for about 10 rows. You are now ready to add the second colour.

5

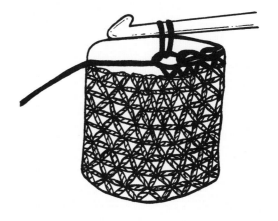

Begin working with a contrasting yarn but don't cut the end of the first one, just weave in the two ends.

6

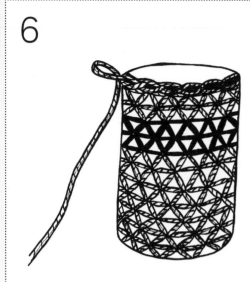

Work 2–3 rows to create a contrasting stripe, then switch back to the original yarn until you have completed around 20 rows in total, depending on your bottle shape.

7

Row 21: Begin to decrease. Make 12 dc then work 2 dc together, then make another 11 dc and 2 dc together.
Row 22: Work all dc as they are.

8

Row 23: From now on you have to crochet with the bottle inserted because your work needs to fit snugly. Work 11 dc then work 2 dc together, then make another 10 dc and 2 dc together.

Row 24: Work all dc as they are.

9

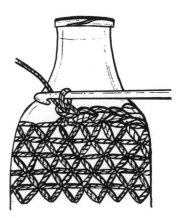

Depending on your bottle shape, you won't have to decrease any more, or you might have to repeat the previous step, reducing the number of dcs. Work another 6 rows (or more, if needed) in dc until you have covered the bottle neck. For the last row use slip stitch. Close the last stitch and, with a smaller hook, take the end of the rope under the cover.

CARPENTER-SQUARE SHELF
BY FABIEN CAPPELLO

Fabien Cappello is a London-based furniture and product designer who cites his main inspiration as the mundanity of daily life. Taking the time to observe our environments and how we inhabit them, he puts the user at the heart of all his designs, regardless of whether these are objects, furniture or spaces. He has a strong interest in both craft techniques and light industrial production, and in his studio there is no contradiction between these approaches, as he employs industrial processes to produce carefully crafted objects.

Fabien does not limit himself to any particular materials, techniques or applications either, describing himself as inherently curious and keen to apply analytical thinking to new challenges. Driven by excitement and optimism, his work is a strong reaction against today's 'disposable' culture and often makes use of upcycled materials to create durable and significant objects — for example, the furniture he makes from recycled Christmas trees. In London alone, over a million trees are thrown away every year, so Fabien makes use of this annual mass disposal of free wood to create a range of stools and tables.

The Carpenter Square Shelf depends on sourcing two identical, flat steel carpenter squares (an L-shaped metal measuring tool). You might be lucky enough to find two squares of identical size from a thrift shop or flea market. Otherwise these can be purchased from any hardware shop.

fabiencappello.com

CARPENTER-SQUARE SHELF

MATERIALS
- ↑ 2 identical, flat steel carpenter squares (the longest side of the square is called the blade; the shorter side is the tongue)
- ↑ 2 x 150cm (60in)-long boards, cut from e.g. solid wood, block boards or plywood, approximately 2cm (¾in) thick (see note below)
- ↑ 10 brass round-head wood screws, 3.5 x 40mm (⅛ x 1½in)
- ↑ 2 flat-head wood screws, 3.5 x 40mm (⅛ x 1½in)
- ↑ 2 wall-mounting plates and appropriate fixings

TOOLS
- ↑ Drill
- ↑ Drill bit for metal, 4mm (⅙in)
- ↑ Drill bit for wood, 2mm (¹⁄₁₂in)
- ↑ Screwdriver

A thickness of around 2cm (¾in) for the boards will ensure the shelf is not too hefty or too flimsy. The width of one board will need to match the short side of the square; the width of the other board will need to match the longer side plus the thickness of the first board. So, for a square with a 20cm (7¾in) tongue and 30cm (11¾in) blade, you would need one board of W20 x L150 x D2cm (7¾ x 60 x ¾in) and another of W28 x L150 x D2cm (11 x 60 x ¾in).

1

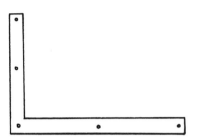

Drill a 4mm (⅙in)-diameter hole 10mm (⅜in) in from each end of both carpenter squares, and a hole 10mm (⅜in) in from each corner. You don't need to measure as the dimensions are already printed on the square! Now drill a hole in the middle of both tongues and blades, an equal distance between the other holes.

2

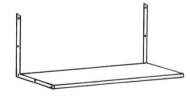

Put the narrower board on a flat surface and place a carpenter square at each end, standing it up on the tongue (short side) and facing the same direction. The depth of the board should match the length of the tongue.

3

Use a pencil to mark the edge of the boards through the holes in the carpenter square. Drill 2mm (1/12in) holes through the centre of the marks.

4

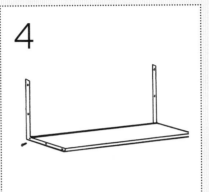

Fasten the squares into each end of the board with round-head screws.

5

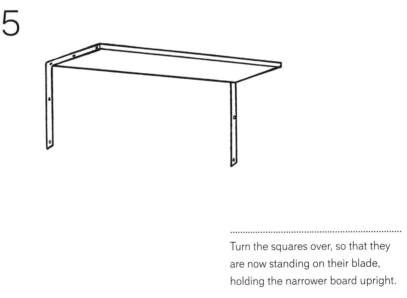

Turn the squares over, so that they are now standing on their blade, holding the narrower board upright.

6

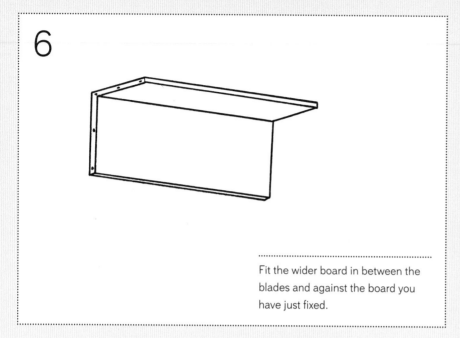

Fit the wider board in between the blades and against the board you have just fixed.

7

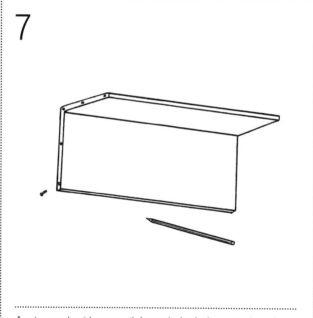

Again, mark with a pencil through the holes onto the edge of the wider board. Drill 2mm (1/12in) holes in the wood at the centre of the marks. Fasten the squares into each side of the board using screws.

8

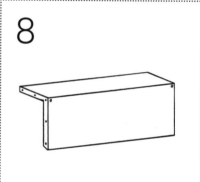

Drill 2mm (1/12in) holes 50cm (19¾in) in from each end of the wider board, into the edge of the narrower board. The holes should be 10mm (⅜in) in from the edge.

9

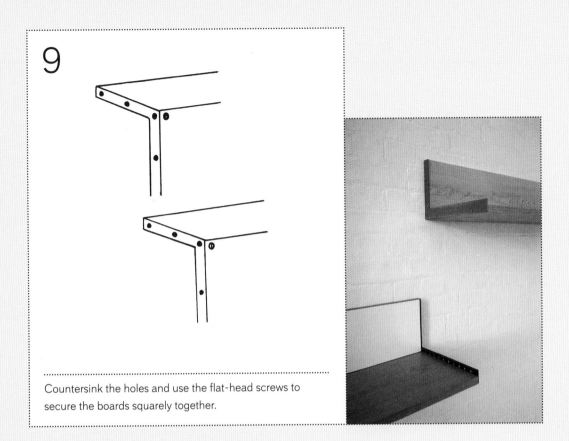

Countersink the holes and use the flat-head screws to secure the boards squarely together.

10

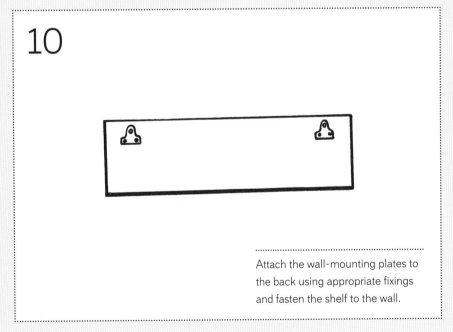

Attach the wall-mounting plates to the back using appropriate fixings and fasten the shelf to the wall.

CRATE STOOL
BY SEGEV MOISA

Segev Moisa was born in Israel and his studio is based in Tel Aviv, but he also spent much of his childhood in Canada. He believes that growing up in these two very different cultures has influenced him greatly and enriched his outlook as a designer. He has also travelled extensively and continues to be inspired by his experiences of diverse cultures and ways of life.

Segev has a passion for hands-on work, and believes that allowing ideas to evolve through physical investigation, rather than attempting to work things out on paper, produces the most meaningful designs. He enjoys working with a wide range of media and tools, but is particularly drawn to recycled materials, both because it makes good sense to use free resources and because he has always been interested — sometimes obsessively — in finding 'stuff' on the streets. This can take the form of an appealing object, something that offers him an interesting material or an item that provides a starting-point for a future project.

Used objects carry a history — a 'life's footprints embedded within their genes' — and tapping into this enables Segev to connect with an object and help it on its way to becoming something desirable again.

The Crate Stool upcycles a discarded plastic crate into a piece of furniture using a traditional weaving technique. Segev uses natural seaweed cord, traditionally used for stools in the Middle East, but it is possible to use any kind of cord. In fact, he says, working with an industrially made cord would definitely be easier!

segevmoisa.com

CRATE STOOL

MATERIALS
↑ Plastic crate (a square crate
  is easier to work with than a
  rectangular one)
↑ Wood scraps (lengths)
↑ Cord rope, seaweed cord or rush

TOOLS
↑ Saw, hacksaw or jigsaw
↑ Drill or Stanley (utility) knife
↑ Spring clamps

1

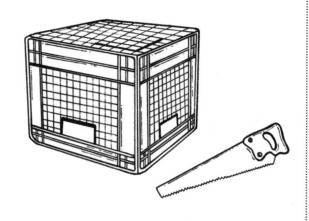

Using a saw, hacksaw or jigsaw, cut out the bottom of the crate, leaving a border of about 5cm (2in).

2

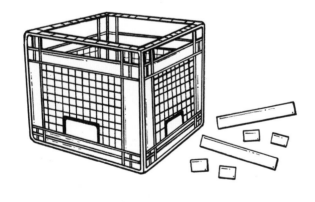

Cut 4cm (1⅝in)-wide slits along each side of the crate near the bottom (the part which will now be the seat). This can be done by drilling a hole and cutting out the rest with a jigsaw. If you don't have these tools, a bit of perseverance with a Stanley knife would work too. Don't cut through the ribs, as these give your crate structural strength.

3

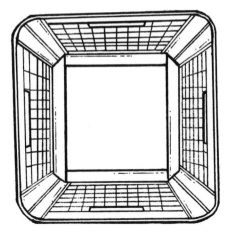

Make a square frame to fit between the slits and the seat. This is just 4 lengths of wood nailed or screwed together at the corners and doesn't need to be pretty as it won't be seen in the end, but it needs to fit snugly. This reinforces the structure and protects it from the tension the weaving will put it under. The crate is now ready for weaving.

4

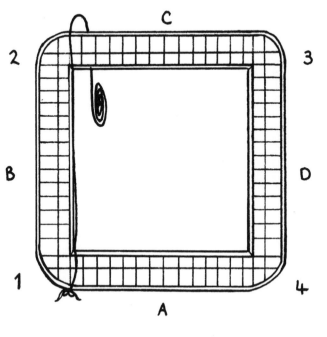

Tip: If you're using seaweed cord, soak it in room-temperature water for 10–15 minutes. This will make it more flexible and prevent the fibres breaking.

Referring to the diagram, tie the end of the cord around beam A and close to leg 1, making sure the knot is hidden inside the crate. If the cord is in a ball, it won't fit through the cut in the side, so unravel a good length of cord and cut it off. When this runs out, simply tie on a new piece, again making sure the knot is hidden underneath.

5

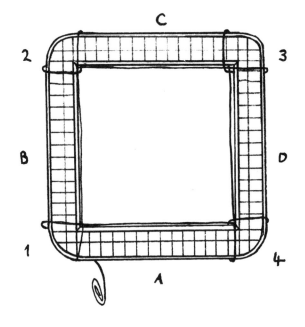

Now pull the cord from A towards beam C around and into the slit beneath it. The cord is now coming out of the middle of the crate, making a 90 degree turn towards beam B, going around the beam, out through the slit and heading in a direct line towards beam D. Pull it over and around the beam, out the slit and turn 90 degrees towards beam C, over the beam, into the slit and straight towards beam A. Turn 90 degrees towards beam D, straight towards beam B, then 90 degrees to A. This completes one turn and brings the cord back to the start.

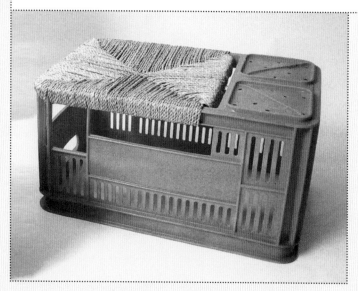

6

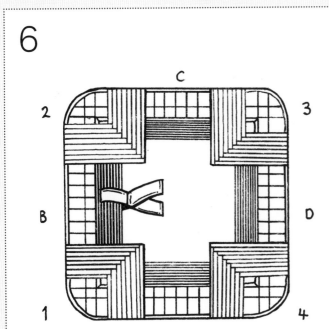

Keeping constant tension on the cord, repeat this process, working round and round. Using spring clamps to hold the cord tight will allow you to rest your hands. Every four or five rounds, push the cords on the beams in towards the legs, beam A towards legs 1 and 4, etc. This is important as it keeps the cords parallel to each other and avoids making a wedge-shaped spacing in the weaving. This will make more sense once you start working.

7

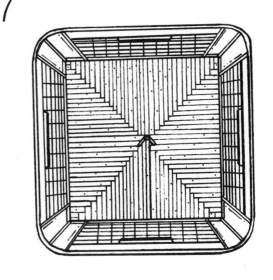

When you reach the centre, tie the final end into the centre, on the inside.

HUNTER LEATHER-LABEL RUG
BY JOANNE CROCKER

Before establishing her label Trash Garden, Joanne Crocker worked as a product developer and homeware buyer. Working with large companies, the Sydney-based designer was astonished by the incredible amount of waste they produced, as well as the lack of eco-friendly production techniques. This experience made her resolve that her own work would never fall into the same trap of unnecessary consumption.

Joanne believes good design should encompass an interesting use of well-thought-out materials and an efficient use of space, be of high quality and function well according to its use. She feels there is no value in an item that looks good if it breaks or wears out in the first year and contends that we must move away from the idea of disposable designs and products.

Trash Garden's products aim to take a more considered approach to design and reflect Joanne's passion for finding new uses for old objects, such as ringpulls from drinks cans. These are turned into bags and accessories by Mexican craftswomen using ringpulls purchased from schools, where they are collected by pupils. The proceeds are then used to provide disabled children with wheelchairs.

The Hunter Leather-Label Rug is made in India using hundreds of reclaimed leather labels collected from denim jeans. Obviously these are challenging to collect in large quantities and they could be replaced by leather remnants cut to size instead. Joanne stresses that the beauty of upcycled products is that no two pieces are alike, so don't be afraid to take this as a starting point and create something different!

upcyclestudio.com.au

HUNTER LEATHER-LABEL RUG

MATERIALS
↟ Leather labels reclaimed from
  jeans, or similar leather pieces
↟ Strong yarn (jute or a thick
  cotton yarn would be fine)
↟ A piece of industrial felt, cut to
  desired rug size
↟ Fabric glue

TOOLS
↟ Leather needle
↟ Craft knife or sharp scissors
↟ Industrial sewing-machine
  (optional)

1

Lay out the leather labels or cut scraps and arrange them into the desired size and layout for your rug. Feel free to trim them down slightly to create the perfect configuration and ensure each one fits snugly against the next. Take a photo of the layout to refer to once you start constructing the rug.

2

Using a leather needle and a strong, heavy yarn, start from the left-hand corner and stitch the first two labels together. If you're looking for uniformity in the finished result, be careful to ensure your stitches are consistent. The easiest technique is to use straight stitches that are parallel to each other, but you could also experiment with various stitching types for different effects.

3

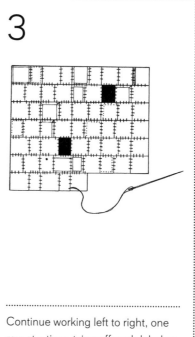

Continue working left to right, one row at a time, tying off each label as it's finished until they are all sewn into place.

4

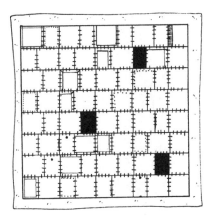

Cut the felt to size. Lay the rug right side up on the felt, then either trim around the edge with a knife or trace the outline with a pen and cut it out with scissors. This example uses a thin, dense felt to create a firm, stable finish that can stand up to being walked on. The felt layer gives the rug stability, body and cushioning, as well as creating a neat backing.

5

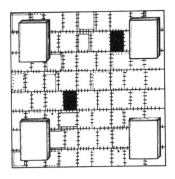

Apply a thin layer of glue to the felt, covering the entire area as evenly as possible. Lay the leather on the felt and align the edges before pressing the pieces together. Lay some heavy books or similar weights on top to ensure firm and even pressure.

6

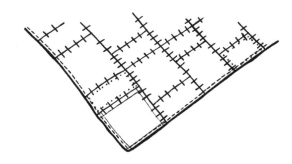

The last step is to finish the perimeter of the rug to ensure the two layers stay together under regular foot traffic. The best method is to run an industrial sewing-machine around the entire rug, but if you don't have access to one of these, you could handstitch the edge with the leather needle used earlier. Create a different look using either blanket stitch or a straight stitch.

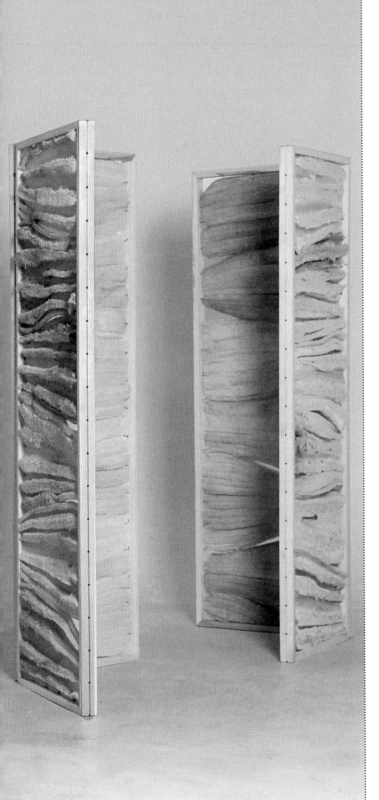

LOOFAH SCREEN
BY FERNANDO LAPOSSE

Fernando Laposse is a Mexican designer, based in London, who tries to push the boundaries of design, gastronomy and the visual arts. As well as working with standard resources such as wood, concrete and metal, he frequently experiments with natural fibres like loofah, and edible materials including sugar, squid ink and egg yolks.

Part of his attraction to unconventional materials is accepting the challenge of doing something beautiful and unexpected with them. He is particularly keen on upcycling and appreciates the magic and amazement it can bring to everyday objects and materials. He also believes that this approach is key to developing a new aesthetic that is not necessarily influenced by current trends — as he puts it, there is 'a lot of design that is well made and tasteful, but in the end it gets lost in the mountains of stuff that look similar to it.'

Fortunately, Fernando's range of products made from loofahs seem unlikely to suffer this fate. Loofah is the edible fruit from a vine related to pumpkins and cucumbers; it grows vertically, attaching itself to trees. Once the fruit is dried and harvested, it is mostly sold for use as an exfoliating body sponge. Fernando's designs explore its lesser-known qualities — lightness, translucency, heat insulation, texture and shock absorption — in products such as lamps, tableware and this room-dividing screen.

This is a fairly simple project for anyone used to working with their hands. Fernando's one note is that although loofah is very cheap and abundant in tropical countries, it may be more expensive and difficult to find in colder climates. Sometimes, though, it can be found fresh at farmer's markets and organic shops, enabling you to strip and dry the fruit yourself.

www.fernandolaposse.com

LOOFAH SCREEN

MATERIALS
- ↑ Approximately 10m (32ft) of 2.5 x 5cm (1 x 2in) wood — enough to make 4 x 1.8m (6ft) lengths and 4 x 60cm (2ft) lengths
- ↑ 12 large loofahs, the bigger the better. These will determine the width of the screen
- ↑ 5m (16ft) of thin polyester thread in a colour that will blend well with the loofahs
- ↑ 10m (32ft) of 3mm (⅛in) polyester thread in any colour
- ↑ 2 brass hinges (optional)

TOOLS
- ↑ Drill
- ↑ Router, chisel or knife
- ↑ Serrated knife
- ↑ Large sewing needle

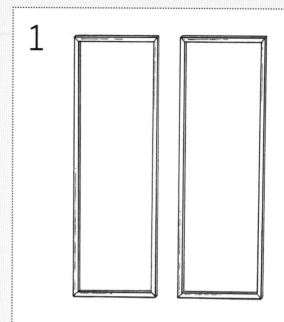

1

Make 2 wooden frames of approximately 180 x 60cm (6 x 2ft). Our example is constructed from maple. Make sure the 5cm (2in) sides of the wood face each other.

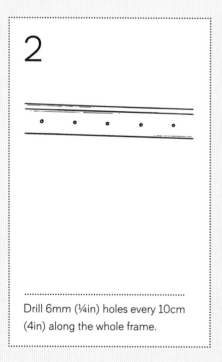

2

Drill 6mm (¼in) holes every 10cm (4in) along the whole frame.

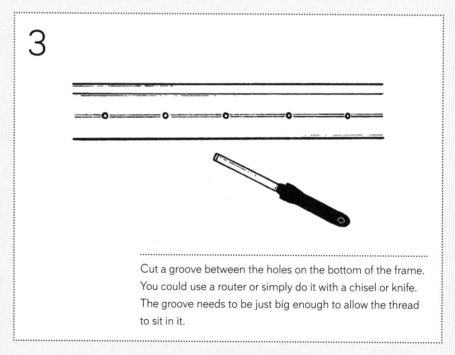

3

Cut a groove between the holes on the bottom of the frame. You could use a router or simply do it with a chisel or knife. The groove needs to be just big enough to allow the thread to sit in it.

4

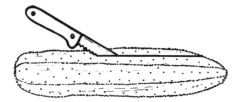

Using a serrated knife, make a slit along the length of each of the loofahs.

5

Wet the loofahs to soften them and force them open (almost as if you were filleting a fish). Lay them out to dry flat with something heavy such as a book on top to prevent them curling back into their original shape. Make sure your weight won't be damaged by the water.

6

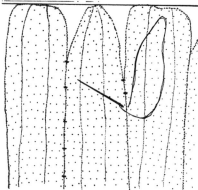

Lay all the flat loofahs next to each other inside the wooden frames, alternating their directions and marking where they touch. You may need to trim away any rough edges. Then make a discreet stitch using the thin polyester thread on every mark you made, so that all the loofahs are now attached to one another.

7

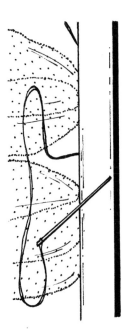

Make a knot on one of the loofahs at the edge and, using the needle, pass the thread through the nearest hole, from the inside of the frame to the outside. Come back from the outside of the next hole and back inside. Pass the needle through the loofah and back out through the same hole. Move on to the next hole and repeat this process all the way round the frame. Be sure to keep the tension consistent, and finish off with a tight knot. Repeat for the other frame.

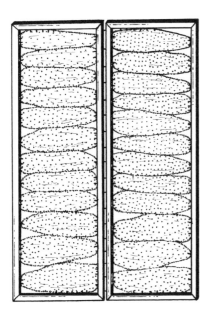

8

Finally, join the frames together, either by creating a hinge between them using the 3mm polyester thread, or simply by screwing on a pair of brass hinges.

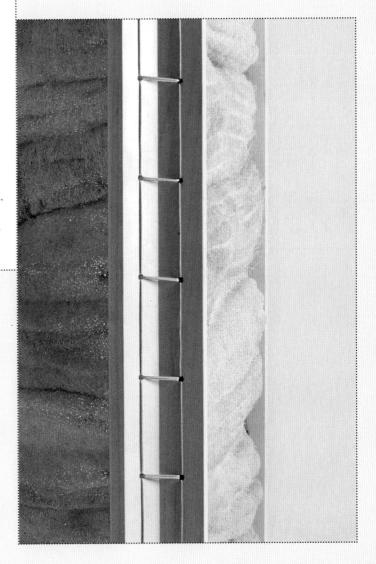

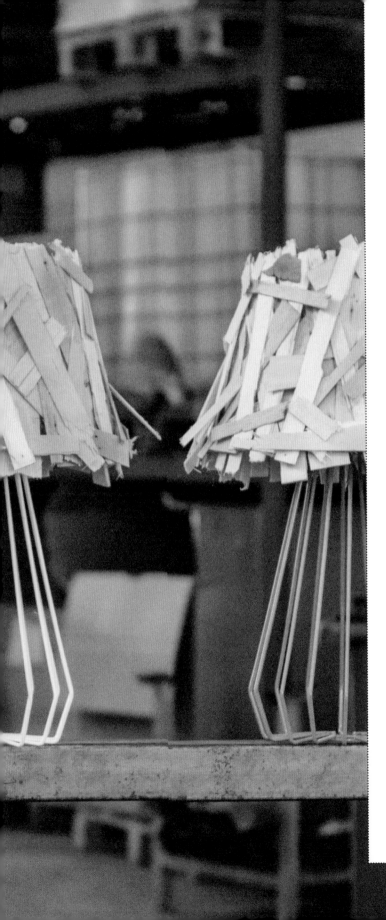

PALITOS LAMP
BY SERGIO MENDOZA

Sergio Mendoza describes his work as 'reality-driven and very oriented towards people'. Relying on common sense and an idealistic view of what life should be like, Sergio believes that good design has the power to make people smile. Regardless of whether he is working on designing a sofa, a beach bar, a sports event or a lamp, he feels that as long as people are happy, the rest is easy.

Based in Valencia, Spain, his studio is strongly influenced by local traditional industries and artisans. Sergio takes pleasure in working with what he calls 'noble materials' such as ceramics, wood and metal, which are tactile materials and can be handled easily. He has found himself becoming increasingly bored of technology, screens and the digital world, and moving towards design that has nothing to do with neon, flashy lights and hi-tech.

Upcycling is one way to create experimental designs at this basic level. Given the sheer amount of waste in society, Sergio feels that, as a designer, he has almost a duty to make use of discarded items. Interesting things are constantly being thrown away; these not only provide materials to work with, but ideas too.

The idea for the Palitos Lamp came from the piles of smashed fruit boxes left in marketplaces at the end of every day. These instructions concentrate on the wooden shade of the lamp, as the base is a bit more difficult to DIY. The shade could also be used alone as a pendant lamp with no base.

www.sergio-mendoza.com

PALITOS LAMP

MATERIALS
↑ Wooden fruit crates
↑ Old lamp frame or similar-
   shaped object
↑ Light fitting

TOOLS
↑ Pliers
↑ Gloves
↑ Hot-glue gun

1

Look for fruit crates in supermarkets, markets and greengrocers. Sergio finds that large companies can be difficult to approach, so take boxes from the waste pile and run! If you can establish good relationships with small shops in your neighbourhood, this can be very helpful.

2

Destroy the boxes. Start by removing the staples with pliers. Break up the wood by hand, wearing gloves to avoid splinters, although you may find it helps to use your feet as well. Sort through the pieces. The best part of the boxes is the thin wood used on the bottom, as it lets light through.

3

You will need a mould to construct the lampshade around, and to maintain the desired shape and proportions. This could be an old wire lamp frame or even a vase, bowl or bucket. Choose an object based on the shape you want the end result to have.

4

Bond the pieces together using the glue gun. Bear in mind that the silicone should not be seen, so think about putting it in places where it can be covered with other wood pieces.

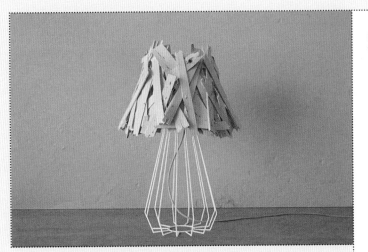

5

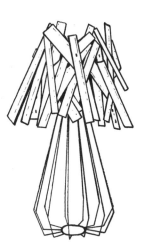

The trick is not to use too much wood, but to be sure there is enough to avoid leaving big holes that let direct light hit your eyes! Test it with a lit bulb from time to time during construction. Attach your light fitting to the shade, and secure it to your base, or suspend it from the ceiling as a pendant.

DIY PANTON CHAIR
BY PETER JAKUBIK

Peter Jakubik is notable for creations that are striking and provocative, yet charged with a sense of humour. The diverse output of the Slovakia-based designer often draws inspiration from fetishes and the idea of 'woman as a designer-erotic object'. He is also keen on the idea of the DIY community and the possibilities of homemade production.

This fondness for the homemade, rather than industrial processes, complements his preference for easily machinable materials such as paper, textiles, wood and leather. Peter has also experimented with recycling scrap wood to make a unique composite material for domestic carpentry projects.

Taking one of the most basic materials imaginable, the DIY Panton Chair is hewn from a solid tree trunk with a skilfully handled chainsaw. Peter incites the public to fabricate their own 'original fake' in homage to Verner Panton's iconic design, explaining mischievously that 'all you need is a picture of the chair, a tree, DIY tools and a passion for designer classics'.

Of course, it is obvious that this approach to the project could only be undertaken by highly skilled individuals with serious tools and safety equipment, as well as access to very large pieces of timber! However, less experienced makers can easily attempt a smaller version, using hand tools and a more modest section of tree. It might take a bit more effort, but soon you too could have what Peter calls a 'genuine copy of the Panton Chair for your holiday cottage or garden party'.

www.peter-jakubik.com

DIY PANTON CHAIR

MATERIALS
↑ Large section of tree trunk without major splits or rot
↑ Finishing oil or wax

TOOLS
↑ Marker pen
↑ Chainsaw and/or handsaw, chisels, gouges, etc.
↑ Chainsaw safety equipment

1

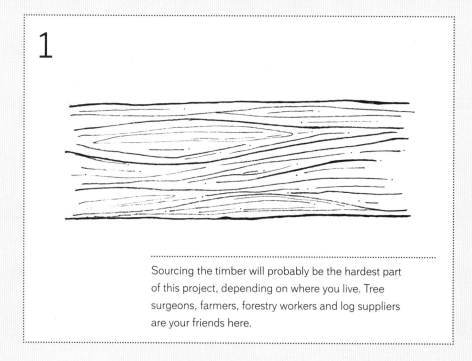

Sourcing the timber will probably be the hardest part of this project, depending on where you live. Tree surgeons, farmers, forestry workers and log suppliers are your friends here.

2

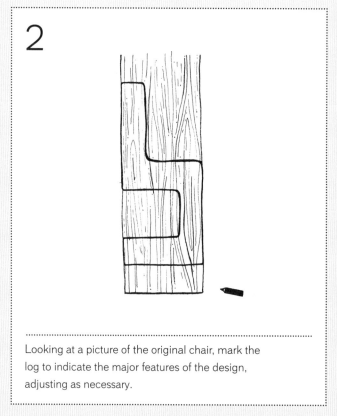

Looking at a picture of the original chair, mark the log to indicate the major features of the design, adjusting as necessary.

3

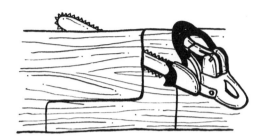

Begin cutting to reveal the shape of the chair. Be as crude or refined as you like, but it is probably worth erring on the side of caution. Mistakes in a piece of timber this size are hard to correct!

4

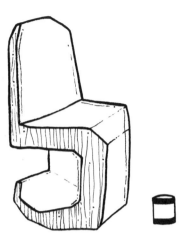

Finish the chair with oil or wax, if desired, to protect the wood and bring out the grain.